Essential Histories

The American Civil War

The war in the West 1863–1865

Essential Histories

The American Civil War

The war in the West 1863–1865

Joseph T Glatthaar

First published in Great Britain in 2001 by Osprey Publishing,
Elms Court, Chapel Way, Botley, Oxford OX2 9LP

Email: info@ospreypublishing.com

ISBN 1 84176 242 3

Editor: Rebecca Cullen
Design: Ken Vail Graphic Design, Cambridge, UK
Cartography by The Map Studio
Index by Alan Thatcher
Picture research by Image Select International
Origination by Grasmere Digital Imaging, Leeds, UK
Printed and bound in China by L. Rex Printing Company Ltd

01 02 03 04 05   10 9 8 7 6 5 4 3 2 1

For a complete list of titles available from Osprey Publishing
please contact:

Osprey Direct UK, PO Box 140,
Wellingborough, Northants, NN8 4ZA, UK
Email: info@ospreydirect.co.uk

Osprey Direct USA,
c/o Motorbooks International, PO Box 1,
Osceola, WI 54020-0001, USA.
Email: info@ospreydirectusa.com

www.ospreypublishing.com

Contents

Introduction

During his Gettysburg Address in November 1863, President Abraham Lincoln reminded his listeners that in 1776, people had come together to form a new nation, one 'conceived in liberty and dedicated to the proposition that all men are created equal.' Eighty-five years later, their descendants fought a great civil war to ensure 'that the nation shall, under God, have a new birth of freedom, and that government of the people, by the people, for the people, shall not perish from the earth.' The American Civil War was, in fact, a struggle over the final draft of both the Declaration of Independence and the United States Constitution, to define freedom and to settle the longstanding dispute over the compatibility of slavery and the purpose of the nation.

By the time of Lincoln's speech, the war had assumed an entirely new dimension. Initially, men on both sides had rushed to arms, fearful of missing out on the great event of their lives. In time, the savagery and the bloodshed, the hunger and the cold, the disease and the death, had altered all that. Banished were naive notions of a short war, a single, decisive battle to prove who was superior. Gone, too, were foolish assumptions about the individual's ability to transform the battlefield. The reality of 1860s warfare, with massive armies using rifled weapons and sustained by the fruits of 1860s industrialization and mechanization, had stripped away much of the glory. Only the starkness and brutality remained. Yet, somehow, those lofty goals that Lincoln had proclaimed still lived in the hearts and minds of the people. Despite hardships, suffering, and losses, soldiers and civilians clung tightly to their cause.

Although the Rebels never had someone whose words so elegantly encapsulated their cause as Lincoln's did, Southern whites also clung to their cause with deep passion. They had seceded to protect the institution of slavery, bequeathed to them by their ancestors. Secessionists may have voiced their cause in words of freedom and rights, but the rights they believed that the Lincoln administration would threaten were their right to own slaves, their right to take those slaves as property into the territories, and their right to live with those slaves in the security that fellow countrymen would not incite those slaves to insurrection. In comparing his new nation to the United States, Vice President of the Confederate States of America Alexander Stephens explained its purpose best when he declared, 'Our new government is founded upon exactly the opposite idea; its foundations are laid, its cornerstone rests, upon the great truth that the negro is not equal to the white man; that slavery ... is his natural and normal condition.'

Northerners, by contrast, rallied around the flag for the lofty goal of preserving the Union. They believed that the Union was inviolate, and that the Republican candidate Abraham Lincoln had won the presidential election fairly. If they accepted the right to secession, Northerners argued, then how could any people ever preserve a democratic republic? Implicit in the Constitution, and understood by every one of the Founding Fathers, was the concept that all Americans must respect the outcome of a fair election. If a minority feared the results of the election, Northerners justified, then its supporters could rely on the system of checks and balances in the Constitution to secure and protect their rights.

By 1863, Lincoln had helped to provide something more tangible to the Union war aims than the sanctity of the Union. He signed the Emancipation Proclamation on New Year's Day, which granted freedom to all slaves in Confederate-held territory. Back in 1858, Lincoln had proclaimed his belief that 'this government cannot endure, permanently half *slave* and half *free.*' While he did not divine civil war, he did predict:

Either the opponents of slavery, will arrest the further spread of it, and place it where the public mind shall rest in the belief that it is in the course of ultimate extinction; or its advocates will push it forward, till it shall become alike lawful in all the States, old as well as new, North as well as South.

Slavery was incompatible with Northern versions of freedom. Based on his constitutional powers as commander in chief, Lincoln decreed that if the Union won, its people could rest assured that they had sowed the seeds for slavery's destruction.

The Emancipation Proclamation also converged with a new approach to warfare that had begun to surface, particularly in the west. Two Federal generals, Ulysses S. Grant and William Tecumseh Sherman, had exchanged ideas on the problems and the conduct of the war. From these communications emerged the rudiments of a new approach to the war, a raiding strategy that would target Confederate civilians and property, in addition to their soldiers, as the enemy. Federal armies would seize slaves, confiscate food and animals, destroy railroads, factories, mills, and anything else of military value, and demonstrate to Confederate soldiers in the ranks just how vulnerable their loved ones were. 'They cannot be made to love us,' Sherman justified to Grant, 'but may be made to fear us, and dread the passage of troops through their country.'

Hardened veterans, too, had replaced raw recruits as the dominant force in these armies. Those who had survived the first two years had formed a different perspective on the war. Like Grant and Sherman, Northern veterans discarded outmoded notions about respect for private property and about treating delicately Southern civilians who supported the men in Rebel uniform. They wanted secessionists to feel the hard hand of war. Confederates, too, had toughened physically, mentally, and emotionally. Unfortunately for them, they had to exhibit that change on battlefields alone. Rarely did they have an opportunity to give Northern civilians a taste of the real war.

Ulysses S. Grant rose from relative obscurity to be the commanding general of the Union armies and directed ultimate Federal victory. His Vicksburg campaign may have been the most brilliant of the war. This photograph, from 1864, was taken during the Overland campaign, when he served as commanding general. (Library of Congress)

Representative of this new attitude was an event that occurred in the last weeks of the fighting, when a Union corps commander arrived at an assigned location a dozen hours behind schedule. Major-General Philip Sheridan promptly ordered his arrest and relieved him from command. Earlier in the war, the Union high command would have celebrated the arrival of a corps in the Eastern Army of the Potomac just 12 hours late. But Sheridan had spent his first three years out west, where a harder breed had emerged as military commanders. They tolerated errors of aggressiveness, not those of caution or tardiness. That spirit in the Federal western armies had begun to infuse soldiers in the east as well.

This, the fourth volume on the American Civil War in the Osprey Essential Histories series, highlights this vital transformation. The book embraces the Western Theater, where Ulysses S. Grant rose to prominence and where Union armies developed an unstoppable momentum. The volume opens with the conclusion of the Vicksburg campaign, perhaps the most masterly of the entire war. It focuses on the burgeoning partnership between Grant and Sherman and their rise to power and influence over the Union war effort. Ultimately, the war in the west came under Sherman's direction, and he left his distinct mark on the way Federal armies would conduct their campaigns. At the same time, these soldiers from the west had their own vision of the way the Union needed to fight this war, and by their conduct they forced their views on officers and men. With the Federal stalemate in the east, this successful collaboration in the west assured Lincoln's re-election and guaranteed four more years of war, if necessary.

For the Federals, too, this volume witnesses the decline of a slow yet capable commander, Major-General William Rosecrans, who committed a blunder based on faulty information, and the rise of a talented replacement, Major-General George H. Thomas, whose stellar service saved the army that day. Thomas continued to earn accolades for his generalship throughout the war, culminating in his decisive victory at Nashville.

On the Confederate side in the Western Theater, no Robert E. Lee emerged. Neither Braxton Bragg, Joseph E. Johnston, nor John Bell Hood proved themselves even pale imitations. Disastrous infighting at the highest levels of the army undermined fine Confederate soldiery, and by the end of the war, Federals had marched right through the heart of the Confederacy and accepted surrender in central North Carolina, not far from Raleigh.

While Abraham Lincoln accomplished his principal goals – the restoration of the Union and the destruction of slavery – he never fully witnessed those achievements. An assassin's bullet struck him down just days after Lee's surrender and almost two weeks before Johnston capitulated in North Carolina. Without Lincoln at the helm, his dream of a new freedom was only partially realized. The United States largely embraced the direction that Northerners had staked out, but it would be another century before African-Americans began to share fully in the rights and benefits of the Republic.

Chronology

1863   **1 January** Lincoln issues the Emancipation Proclamation
2 January Second day of fighting at Stones River
16 April Porter's flotilla runs past Vicksburg batteries
17 April Colonel Benjamin Grierson begins his 600-mile (965km) raid from La Grange, Tennessee, through Mississippi to help Grant's army
30 April Porter ferries part of Grant's army across the Mississippi River
1 May Grant defeats Confederates at Port Gibson, Mississippi
2 May Grierson's raiders reach Baton Rouge, Louisiana
12 May Grant defeats Confederates at Raymond, Mississippi
14 May Grant drives Johnston's forces back from Jackson, Mississippi
16 May Grant defeats Pemberton at Champion Hill
17 May Grant defeats Pemberton at Big Black River
19 May Grant's first assault on Vicksburg fails
22 May Grant's second assault fails; he lays siege
27 May Banks attacks, besieges Port Hudson; first major engagement for black soldiers
7 June Confederate attack on Milliken's Bend
11 June Banks's attack repulsed at Port Hudson
14 June Banks's attack repulsed for third time at Port Hudson
23 June Rosecrans advances on Tullahoma, Tennessee
3 July Bragg retreats to Chattanooga, Tennessee
4 July Pemberton surrenders Vicksburg to Grant

9 July Port Hudson surrenders to Banks
19 July Union attack on Fort Wagner, led by 54th Massachusetts (Colored) Infantry
15 August Burnside begins campaign for Knoxville, Tennessee
16 August Rosecrans begins campaign for Chattanooga
21 August Quantrill's raid on Lawrence, Kansas
2 September Burnside occupies Knoxville
9 September Rosecrans occupies Chattanooga
18 September Longstreet's men begin to reinforce Bragg's army
19 September Battle of Chickamauga, Tennessee, begins
20 September Longstreet breaks Rosecrans's line
23 September Bragg lays siege of Chattanooga
24 September Hooker leaves for Chattanooga with XI and XII Corps
17 October Grant made commander of all Union forces in the west
19 October Thomas replaces Rosecrans
23 October Grant arrives at Chattanooga
4 November Longstreet detached to attack Burnside at Knoxville
20 November Sherman arrives at Chattanooga with reinforcements
23 November Thomas seizes Orchard Knob
24 November Hooker drives Confederates off Lookout Mountain
25 November Sherman's attack stalls; Thomas's men storm Missionary Ridge
29 November Longstreet repulsed by Burnside at Knoxville

1 December Bragg resigns as Army of Tennessee commander
27 December Johnston assumes command of Army of the Tennessee

1864 **3 February** Sherman leaves Vicksburg on Meridian campaign
4 March Sherman completes Meridian campaign
12 March Grant promoted to lieutenant-general
18 March Sherman assumes command of Union forces in the west
25 March Banks begins Red River campaign
8 April Banks defeated by Richard Taylor at Sabine Crossroads, Louisiana
12 April Forrest's massacre of black soldiers at Fort Pillow, Tennessee
6 May Sherman opens Atlanta campaign
9 May McPherson's flanking movement stalls
13–16 May Battle of Resaca
18 May Battle of Yellow Bayou, Louisiana, the last battle of the Red River campaign
19 May Johnston's attack at Cassville never develops
24 May Sherman outflanks Johnston's position at Allatoona, Georgia
25–27 May Battle around Dallas, Georgia
8 June Lincoln renominated for president
14 June Lieutenant-General Leonidas Polk killed at Pine Mountain
27 June Sherman's assault on Kennesaw Mountain repulsed
4–9 July Sherman maneuvers across Chattahoochee River
17 July Hood replaces Johnston as commander of Army of the Tennessee
20 July Hood repulsed at Peachtree Creek
22 July Hood fails to turn Sherman's army at Battle of Atlanta; Major-General James B. McPherson is killed
28 July Hood's attack at Ezra Church repulsed

5 August Farragut wins Battle of Mobile Bay
29 August McClellan nominated for president
31 August Battle of Jonesboro, Georgia
1 September Battle of Jonesboro concluded; Hood evacuates Atlanta
2 September Sherman occupies Atlanta
19 September Price with 12,000 men crosses into Missouri
27 September Anderson's attack on Centralia, Missouri
28 September Hood moves to strike at Sherman's supply line
October Hood fails to capture Allatoona; Sherman in pursuit
18 October Hood crosses into Alabama
23 October Price defeated at Westport; begins retreat
30 October Sherman shifts Schofield's troops to support Thomas in Middle Tennessee
8 November Lincoln re-elected
15 November Sherman's troops burn Atlanta; begin March to the Sea
19 November Hood opens push into Middle Tennessee
23 November Milledgeville, capital of Georgia, falls to Sherman
29 November Schofield escapes at Spring Hill, Tennessee
30 November Schofield repulses Hood at Franklin; Lieutenant-General Patrick Cleburne killed
2 December Hood besieges Nashville
13 December Sherman captures Fort McAllister
15–16 December Thomas routs Hood's army
21 December Sherman occupies Savannah
25 December Butler repulsed at Fort Fisher, North Carolina

1865 **15 January** Fort Fisher falls to Porter and Terry; Hood relieved of command of Army of the Tennessee

31 January Thirteenth Amendment abolishing slavery passes in Congress
1 February Sherman begins Carolinas campaign
17 February Columbia falls to Sherman, burns
18 February Charleston seized by Union troops
22 February Wilmington surrenders to Schofield; Johnston recalled to command Confederate forces against Sherman
4 March Lincoln's Second Inauguration
16 March Sherman pushes back Hardee at Averasborough, North Carolina
17 March Major-General E. R. S. Canby attacks Mobile, Alabama
19–21 March Sherman repulses Johnston's attack at Bentonville, North Carolina
24 March Sherman occupies Goldsboro, North Carolina, ending the Carolinas campaign
28 March Lincoln, Grant, Sherman, and Porter confer on peace terms

3 April Richmond falls
8 April Sherman resumes march on Johnston
9 April Lee surrenders to Grant at Appomattox Court House
12 April Mobile falls to Canby; Johnston tells President Jefferson Davis resistance is hopeless
13 April Raleigh falls to Sherman
14 April Lincoln shot at Ford's Theater
15 April Lincoln dies; Andrew Johnson succeeds as president
18 April Sherman and Johnston sign broad surrender agreement
21 April President Johnson and cabinet reject Sherman's terms
26 April Johnston accepts same terms as Grant gave Lee
10 May President Davis is captured at Irwinsville, Georgia
13 May Last battle of the war, at Palmito Ranch, Texas
23–24 May Grand Review in Washington, DC
26 May General Edward Kirby Smith surrenders Confederate forces west of the Mississippi River

War takes its toll

When the war broke out, the Northern states possessed a vast superiority of resources, so much so that some scholars have depicted Confederate efforts at independence as doomed from the start. That argument, however, draws on the critical knowledge that the Confederacy ultimately lost. In wartime, nations must be able to tap their resources, to convert them into military strength, and to focus and sustain that force at the enemy's critical source of power, what Prussian military theorist Carl von Clausewitz called the center of gravity. The task is easier said than done. In an industrialized world, it takes prolonged periods to mobilize manpower, to convert manufacturing to wartime purposes, and to replace valuable personnel who have rushed off to arms but who had produced on farms and in factories. Then, political and uniformed leaders must map out strategy, train and equip armies, and finally oversee the successful execution of military operations.

Certainly the advantage of resources rested with the Federals. Four of every five white persons lived in the Northern states, and the region held 90 percent of all manufacturing. The Union was home to two of every three farms, and possessed a modern and efficient transportation system.

But the Confederacy had advantages as well. The seceding states encompassed over 700,000 square miles (1.8 million km²) of territory. Since the Union sought to conquer the Rebels, its armed forces must overcome a hostile people over an enormous land mass. That huge Southern coastline – some 3,500 miles (5,600km) – no doubt could serve as an avenue of invasion. At the same time, it also offered easy access for imported goods, which could compensate for limited manufacturing capabilities. The Confederacy had a well-educated segment of the population who could design and build factories. And while the North had an overwhelming advantage in population, the Confederacy hoped to rely on three and a half million slaves. Their labors could offset the loss of productivity when white men took up arms and actually enable the Confederate states to place a higher proportion of their population in uniform.

After 27 months of fighting, Union armies had seized control of the Mississippi River, severing the Confederacy and reducing further contributions to the area west of the river to a trickle. Grant alone had captured two Rebel armies, totaling nearly 50,000. Federal forces had secured Kentucky and much of Tennessee, in addition to large portions of Missouri, Mississippi, and Louisiana. Tens of thousands of slaves had flooded Union lines. Early in the war, these laborers had produced for the Confederacy; now, they would work to defeat it. With the Emancipation Proclamation in effect, the Union armies would make a conscientious effort to strip Southerners of their slaves and to recruit them to work for or serve in the Federal armies. As Lincoln assessed pithily to Grant, 'It works doubly – weakening the enemy and strengthening us.'

By mid-1863, too, Northern might had just begun to weigh into the equation. There were twice as many Federals present for duty as Confederates, and the Union could replace its losses much more easily than the Confederacy. These Yankees, moreover, were better clothed, better fed, and better equipped than their Rebel opponents. It took a while, but the preponderance of Union resources began to take effect. Factories in the North churned out enormous quantities of military and civilian products, and imports continued to pour into New York, Boston, Philadelphia, and other port cities.

President Abraham Lincoln struggled to find someone who could exploit the Northern superiority in resources and lead the Union army to victory. Eventually he found that person in Ulysses S. Grant. (National Archives)

of the entire Confederacy for the war. Yankee munitions makers manufactured 50 percent more small-arms cartridges in one year than the Confederacy made for the entire war. Had Confederate ports been open, the Rebels could have offset the imbalance through imports, but Northern shipbuilders crafted ironclads and wooden vessels in such prodigious numbers that the once porous blockade had begun to tighten significantly.

While momentum had shifted to the Federals, two critical questions remained. Would the Union place individuals in high command who would direct the armies and resources skillfully against the Confederate center of gravity – its people's willingness to resist Union authority in order to create an independent nation? Second, would the Northern public and the armies in the field continue to support the cause in the face of huge losses, sacrifices, and hardships?

From the Confederate standpoint, despite losses in manpower and territory in the first 27 months of fighting, most Southern whites retained a powerful commitment to the war. Morale had rolled up and down, based largely on battlefield successes and failures. Still, Confederates realized that the Union had to conquer them to win, and in mid-1863, the secessionists were a long way from being defeated. Most Confederate land remained in Rebel control. No massive slave rebellions had taken place, and although large numbers had fled to the enemy, millions remained behind and produced for the Rebel cause. The primary armies stood intact, and the one in Virginia appeared unbeatable on home soil. No doubt, soldiers and civilians suffered shortages, but Southern farms and factories produced enough to sustain both sectors. If the Confederacy could resist stoutly for another 16 months, till the Northern presidential election, perhaps its people could force a political decision by swaying Northerners into voting a peace party into power.

Relying on farm machinery to offset manpower loss, Northern farmers grew bumper crops, despite inclement weather. And after some initial struggles, Northerners had mastered the art and science of logistics – the supply and transportation of its armies – to ensure that soldiers in the field received much of that productive bounty.

The conversion of Northern industry to wartime production also advantaged the Union. After the war, Confederate Chief of Ordnance Josiah Gorgas boasted that the Confederacy never lost a battle because its armies lacked ammunition. Yet Northern factories churned out vastly more ammunition and weapons, and the quality was superior. The Northern states forged as many field and coastal artillery guns in a single year as did the combined productivity

Overview and final stages

On 1 April 1863, a pleasant yet unimpressive-looking man – medium height, medium build with brown hair and trimmed whiskers – cast his eyes across the Yazoo River in Mississippi at the high ground called Haines' Bluff. It would not work, he concluded sadly.

For six months, Major-General Ulysses Simpson Grant had attempted to seize the Confederate bastion of Vicksburg, located high up on the bluffs overlooking the Mississippi River. He had tried scheme after scheme to get at the Confederate forces there, and each one failed. From this observation point 11 miles (18km) from Vicksburg, Grant realized that an attack here would result in 'immense sacrifice of life, if not defeat.' He had exhausted all options. 'This, then, closes out the last hope of turning the enemy by the right,' he admitted the next day to Admiral David Dixon Porter, Commander of the Mississippi Squadron. He must concentrate on turning the enemy left.

Since Lieutenant-General Winfield Scott, the Union Commanding General early in the war, had prepared his concept for Federal victory – derisively called the 'Anaconda Plan' by the media – control of the Mississippi River had been a top priority. If the Union held the river, it would slice off part of the Confederacy, thereby severing the Eastern Confederacy from the bountiful supply of cattle and horses that Texas possessed and virtually isolating Rebel troops there. Federal forces could move up and down the Mississippi with impunity, launching raids that could penetrate deeply into rebellious states. Once more, too, Midwestern farmers could ship their produce downriver to New Orleans and on to ocean-going vessels for distant markets, providing a cheaper transportation alternative to expensive railroads.

Despite Grant's frustration over Vicksburg, the Union war effort in the west had achieved significant results after two years of fighting. And at the heart of those successes had been that fellow Grant.

After Confederate gunners had fired on Fort Sumter, Federal President Abraham Lincoln called out the militia to put down the rebellion. Virginia, North Carolina, Tennessee, and Arkansas used that as their cue to secede from the Union and join fellow slaveholding states of South Carolina, Florida, Georgia, Alabama, Mississippi, Louisiana, and Texas in the Confederate States of America. They would resist by force of arms any attempt by the old Union to enforce its laws or maintain control of its property.

Four other slaveholding states did not officially join the Confederacy. Delaware, with a tiny slave population, remained solidly pro-Union. The other three, however, were more problematic. Lincoln employed legal and illegal means to keep Maryland from seceding. Missouri erupted in a nasty civil war of its own, and even though the Federals gained dominance there, guerrilla fighting plagued its population for years. The last one, Kentucky, was the worst combination of the other two. The situation in Kentucky was as complicated as Missouri, and its handling required even more delicacy than Maryland.

Early on, Kentucky declared its neutrality. While a majority of the people in that commonwealth probably preferred to remain in the Union, Kentuckians feared that their homes would become the battleground if they declared themselves for either side. Lincoln, who was born in Kentucky, knew just how valuable it was to the Union. He reportedly told someone that, while he hoped to have God on his side, he must have Kentucky. With its large number of livestock, its agriculture, its manufacturing and mining, and its almost 500 miles (800km) of banks along the Ohio River, the Union could not afford a hostile Kentucky. Lincoln raised substantial forces and positioned them to strike into the commonwealth, but only if the Confederacy violated its neutrality first.

Fortunately for Lincoln, he did not have to wait long. In one of the great blunders of the war, Major-General Leonidas Polk, a former West Point classmate of Confederate President Jefferson Davis, who had gone on to become an Episcopal bishop, violated Kentucky neutrality. Fearful that Federals might seize Columbus, Kentucky, Polk ordered its occupation in September 1861. Union Brigadier-General U. S. Grant responded by sending troops to Paducah and Smithland, where the Tennessee and Cumberland Rivers meet the Ohio. The Union-leaning legislature of Kentucky condemned Polk's act and proclaimed that the Confederate invaders must be expelled. By acting with restraint, Lincoln kept Kentucky in Union hands. And it paid great dividends. While some 35,000 Kentuckians served in the Confederate army, 50,000 fought for the Federals.

Leonidas Polk, a West Point graduate and bishop of the Louisiana. Polk violated Kentucky's neutrality in one of the great blunders of the war. As a corps commander, he promoted unrest with Bragg. Polk was killed during the Atlanta campaign. (Library of Congress)

Grant, a West Point graduate with considerable combat experience in the war with Mexico, had grasped the value of aggressiveness in warfare. Two months after his move into Kentucky, he gained his first Civil War combat experience at Belmont, Missouri. Grant's forces surprised a Confederate command there and drove them out of camp. Then, the lack of discipline among Grant's inexperienced troops wreaked havoc. They broke ranks and began plundering, setting themselves up for a Confederate counterattack that drove them back. At Belmont, Grant exhibited dash and recorded an important lesson about the nature of his volunteers.

Grant's first major campaign brought him back to the Tennessee and Cumberland Rivers. The Tennessee River dipped down through Kentucky and Tennessee and into northern Alabama. The Cumberland extended not quite as far south, but it did course through the Tennessee state capital of Nashville. Union control of these rivers would offer excellent naval support for invading armies.

The Confederates, who recognized the value of these waterways, erected forts along both rivers to block Federal movements, but with a huge area stretching from the Appalachian Mountains to southwest Missouri to protect, they lacked the troop strength to repel a large and effectively managed attack – exactly what Grant delivered.

In February 1862, Grant had obtained permission from his superior officer, Major-General Henry Wager Halleck, to transport his command of 15,000, accompanied by naval gunboats, down the Tennessee River and to secure Fort Henry, which blocked waterway traffic and military penetration into central Tennessee. By the time he arrived there, winter rains and ensuing floods had swamped Fort Henry, making it indefensible. Instead, Confederate forces concentrated on firmer ground at Fort Donelson, a dozen miles (19km) east on the banks of the Cumberland River, leaving behind only a paltry garrison of artillerists.

Those remnants at Fort Henry quickly succumbed to US navy shelling.

The new Confederate commander of the Western Department, General Albert Sidney Johnston, had no delusions about the overextended nature of the Confederate defenses. Located at Bowling Green, Kentucky, with about 25,000 troops, Johnston worried that the Federals would pierce his weak cordon and then outflank or trap a large portion of his manpower among Grant's command, a smaller one to the east under Brigadier-General Don Carlos Buell, and the Union river gunboats. After meeting with senior officers, Johnston decided to fall back to a Memphis–Nashville line, but also sent reinforcements to Fort Donelson to delay Grant's advance. Even worse, the two ranking commanders at Donelson were military incompetents yet well-connected politicians, John B. Floyd and Gideon Pillow.

Grant, meanwhile, immediately shifted his focus to the Confederates at Fort Donelson. Unlike so many Union officers, Grant grasped the value of initiative in warfare. He directed two divisions to slog their way through mud to the outskirts of the Confederate positions. The succeeding day, a third division arrived by transport along the Cumberland River, and with the aid of Federal gunboats, Grant invested the Rebel forces.

At Fort Donelson, the Confederates suffered from dreadful leadership. They launched a surprise attack that pried open an escape route, but Pillow grew squeamish over the losses and convinced Floyd to cancel the breakout. Seizing the opportunity, the aggressive Grant launched a counterattack of his own which not only sealed the breakthrough but occupied some vital positions in the old Confederate line as well. Unable to withstand another Federal assault, the Confederate commanders realized that their situation had become hopeless. Floyd fled, followed by Pillow. Also refusing to surrender was a disgusted colonel named Nathan Bedford Forrest, who would prove to be a Union scourge for the next three years. Forrest took 700 horsemen with him.

That left Brigadier-General Simon Bolivar Buckner, an old friend of Grant's, to request terms for capitulation. Grant's terse reply, wholly in character with his approach to warfare, captured the imagination of the Northern public: 'No terms except an unconditional and immediate surrender can be accepted. I propose to move upon your works immediately.' Buckner angrily relented, and Grant had gained the first important Union victory of the war, taking nearly 13,000 Rebels prisoner.

With the fall of Forts Henry and Donelson, the door opened for a rapid advance on Nashville. Grant and Buell both made haste, and by late February the city had fallen into Union hands. Grant's columns then pushed on to the Tennessee River, where they awaited reinforcements for a large-scale advance on Corinth, Mississippi, the site of a major rail intersection.

After abandoning Nashville, Johnston fell back to Corinth. There, he gathered some 40,000 Rebel troops and hatched a scheme to crush Grant's command before it united with Buell. Grant's soldiers, positioned largely on the south side of the Tennessee River, had failed to fortify. An effective Confederate attack might be able to pin the Yankees against the riverbank and crush them. With his army prepared to assail the Union lines the next day, Johnston vowed they would water their horses in the Tennessee River tomorrow.

In the early morning of 6 April, Johnston's troops struck Brigadier-General William Tecumseh Sherman's division, catching them largely without fortifications. Sherman and most of the Federals fought valiantly that day, but the Rebel onslaught was too much. Even though thousands of Federals cowered under the riverbank, Union troops had resisted enough for the Yankees to regroup and prepare a defensive position, aided by ample artillery. There, they received help from portions of Buell's army, which began arriving in the late afternoon. Among the staggering number of casualties, close to 20,000 that April day, was Albert Sidney Johnston, who bled to death from an untreated leg wound.

Major Union campaigns 1863–1865

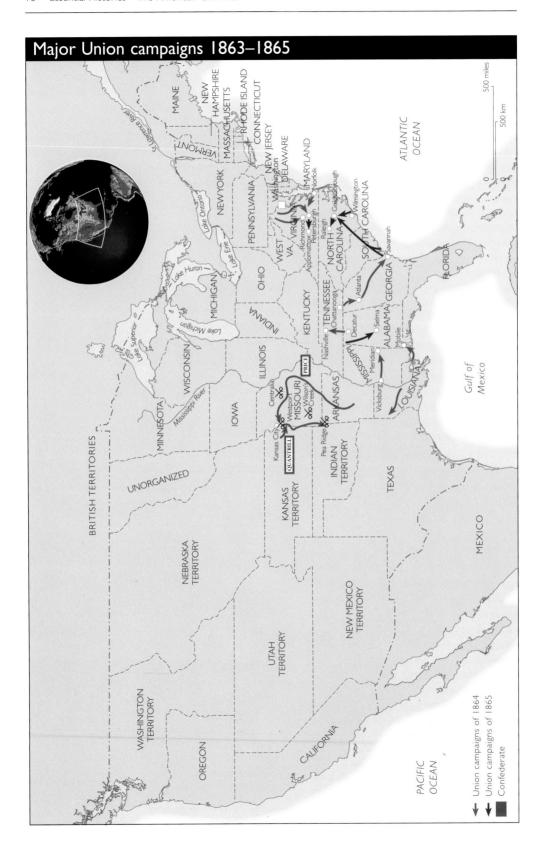

With reinforcements from Buell's command, Grant seized the initiative early the next morning, attacking and eventually sweeping the field by afternoon. Sherman then attempted to organize an effective pursuit, but it was too late. The Federals were as confused in victory as the Rebels were in defeat.

What Grant won on the battlefield at Shiloh, however, he lost in the eyes of the Northern public. The unprepared state of the army, and the massive casualties at Shiloh, over 13,000 on the Union side and 10,600 Confederates in two days, appalled Northerners, and cries for Grant's removal radiated from all around the country. Halleck stepped in, stilling the public clamor against Grant but also displacing him. While Grant stewed in his nominal post of second-in-command, Halleck cautiously maneuvered his ponderous army of over 100,000 and eventually occupied Corinth.

By mid-June 1862, the Union had achieved extraordinary success in the West. Kentucky and central and western Tennessee had fallen into Union hands, as had a part of northern Mississippi. Brigadier-General John Pope had crushed Rebel defenses at New Madrid, Missouri, and Island No. 10, removing obstacles to Mississippi River passage all the way down to northern Mississippi. Naval forces advancing downriver blasted past Fort Pillow, and by early June they had shelled Memphis into submission. Farther to the south, a Union fleet led by David Farragut had pounded its way upriver and compelled the Confederacy's largest city, New Orleans, to surrender. Occupation troops followed.

When Lincoln called Halleck to Washington as commanding general the following month, it looked on the surface as if the Confederacy in the west was in dire straits. But before Halleck left, he slowed the advance and began to consolidate Federal gains, dispersing his massive army for some occupation duty and an advance under Buell on Chattanooga, Tennessee. It did not take long for the initiative to shift to the Confederacy.

Admiral David Farragut became the first great naval hero for the United States in the war. A bold commander, Farragut forced his fleet up the Mississippi River and compelled New Orleans to surrender in 1862. Later, he forced his way into Mobile Bay and closed a valuable Confederate port. (Library of Congress)

After Johnston's death, his second-in-command, General P. G. T. Beauregard, took over. Beauregard successfully evacuated Corinth, but then took an unauthorized leave when he fell ill. Confederate President Davis, already irritated with Beauregard for his unprofessional conduct in Virginia, used this as the basis for Beauregard's replacement. Davis chose General Braxton Bragg, a Mexican War hero with a reputation for quarrelsomeness, as the new commander.

Confederate cavalrymen in the area taught Bragg a valuable lesson. While Buell's army crept east toward Chattanooga, Forrest's cavalry struck his railroad supply line, and later another mounted raid under Kentuckian John Hunt Morgan did so as well. Both Rebel horsemen made Buell's life extremely difficult. Bragg realized that a larger, coordinated movement in the Federal rear might wreak havoc on Federal troops in

Mississippi and Tennessee, and force them to yield the territory they had taken since February. Once Confederate troops trod on Kentucky soil, Bragg was sure thousands would flock to his army and take up arms against the Union.

By rail, Bragg shifted 30,000 men to Chattanooga, where they began an advance. From Knoxville, Tennessee, Edmund Kirby Smith with 21,000 men, including a division of Bragg's, left in mid-August, passing through the Cumberland Gap and driving deep into Kentucky. Yet the march into the Bluegrass State was not much cause for local celebration. Few volunteers rushed to the Rebel banner.

Prodded by military and political officials, Buell finally undertook pursuit in early October. After much maneuvering on both sides, portions of the two armies collided in

The despised commander of the Army of the Tennesssee, Braxton Bragg had been a hero in the Mexican War, where he made a favorable impression on Jefferson Davis. His failure to follow up at Chickamauga may have been one of the greatest mistakes of the war. He resigned command of the army after the débâcle at Missionary Ridge. (Library of Congress)

some hilly terrain around Perryville, Kentucky. Because of an acoustic shadow, neither Bragg nor Buell heard any shots and they did not know the battle was taking place. As a result, soldiers who were literally a few miles from the battlefield did not participate. Despite 7,500 casualties, neither side gained an advantage, and Bragg withdrew his forces back to Tennessee.

The raid into Kentucky exposed serious flaws in both the Confederate and the Union commanders. Grumbling over Bragg filtered back to Richmond, and Confederate President Davis, himself a man of considerable military experience and accomplishment, proposed an interesting solution. General Joseph E. Johnston, who had suffered a serious wound at the Battle of Seven Pines several months earlier, had recovered enough to return to active duty. He could not get his old command back; General Robert E. Lee had been so effective with it that the soldiers and the public viewed the army as his. But Johnston possessed leadership skills and experience that the Confederacy needed. Rather than replace Bragg or the new commander around Vicksburg, Northern-born Lieutenant-General John C. Pemberton, Davis superseded them.

All along, Davis hoped his commanders could assume the offensive, but when the Federals advanced, the Confederate President wanted army commanders to concentrate manpower and other resources by tapping neighboring departments. Johnston's new assignment was to oversee military forces from the Appalachian Mountains to the Mississippi River. Davis expected him to coordinate their military activities, help them formulate plans, inspect, critique, and advise. Of course, when he was present, Johnston should command, but Davis wanted him to focus on the strategic and operational, not the tactical, levels. Johnston never grasped the concept.

Similarly, on the Union side, Lincoln had soured on Buell. Cautious to a fault, Buell followed Bragg hesitantly as the Rebel army escaped from Kentucky. By late October, an exasperated Lincoln had had enough. When Buell announced that he preferred to restore his supply base in Nashville instead of chasing Rebels, the President replaced him with Major-General William Rosecrans.

Lincoln wanted generals who would seize the initiative and, for a while, it appeared as if he had chosen the wrong man. Rosecrans planned painstakingly, and when Lincoln urged him to advance on the enemy, he refused to budge until everything was in order. Finally, Rosecrans moved out of Nashville with 42,000 men the day after Christmas. Despite skillful harassment by Rebel cavalry, Rosecrans pressed on toward Chattanooga and Bragg's army. On 30 December 1862, the armies confronted each other around Stones River, just north of Murfreesboro.

Strangely enough, Rosecrans and Bragg formed the same plan: to turn their opponents' right flank and get in their rear. Bragg got a jump on the Federals the next day, attacking first. His people roared down on the Yankee flank and pushed it back, but the Confederates could not get around Rosecrans's rear. On New Year's Day, the two sides skirmished. On the following day, though, Bragg attacked on the other side of the field. Although his men gained some high ground, they suffered heavy losses from Yankee artillery. As Union reinforcements arrived the next day, Bragg knew he must fall back.

At the Battle of Stones River, Rosecrans suffered 31 percent casualties, while Bragg lost a third of his men. Together, these were the highest proportionate losses in a single, major battle throughout the war. In victory, it took months for Rosecrans's Army of the Cumberland to recover. In defeat, dissension over Bragg worsened, but Johnston refused to take over, fearing the perception of him replacing Bragg with himself.

Farther to the west, Grant's reputation plummeted after the débâcle at Shiloh. When Halleck stepped in to oversee the Corinth campaign, Grant had nothing to do. After pondering for some time, he decided to ask Halleck to relieve him. Fortunately, Sherman talked Grant out of leaving, and six weeks later, authorities ordered Halleck to

Henry W. Halleck, who was Grant's commander during the Forts Henry and Donelson campaign, supplanted him after Shiloh. A critic of Grant, his appointment as commanding general restored Grant to command. He later served under Grant as chief of staff. (Library of Congress)

Washington and appointed him general-in-chief. Grant resumed charge of his old army. Patience had won Grant an opportunity to restore his name.

Back east, too, Grant won a reprieve. Halleck's ascension to the office of general-in-chief in the summer of 1862 improved his standing with the authorities in Washington. The new commanding general arrived in the nation's capital as a moderately strong Grant proponent. Halleck publicly exonerated him for his actions at Shiloh. After his own experiences in command at Corinth, Halleck had softened his initial criticism of Grant. Although he 'is careless of his command,' Halleck commented to Secretary of the Treasury Salmon P. Chase, he evaluated Grant 'as a good general and brave in battle.'

The Vicksburg campaign

For several months afterward, Grant did little but combat raiding parties and guerrilla bands. After Halleck had scattered his mammoth army, Grant lacked sufficient force to launch another offensive. Runaway slaves, cotton trading, guerrillas, Confederate raids, and offended civilians absorbed his time and energy. Campaigning, it seemed, had taken a back seat to occupying secessionist territory.

But by late October 1862, pressure for a campaign against Vicksburg had begun to build. Nestled on a 200ft (61m) bluff overlooking the Mississippi River, Vicksburg dominated passage along the waterway. In Confederate hands, some cleverly positioned cannon could block Union transit. For the Federals, Vicksburg and Port Hudson, Louisiana, represented the last two Rebel strongholds along the Mississippi River. Once Vicksburg fell to Union forces, Port Hudson would become untenable. Then the Federals would control the entire length of the river and would slice off and isolate the Trans-Mississippi Confederacy.

A politician turned general, John A. McClernand, had received authority from Lincoln to raise a command to capture Vicksburg. Grant, who knew McClernand well, had serious doubts about McClernand's ability and temperament to lead such an expedition, judging him 'unmanageable and incompetent,' and at the urging of Halleck he decided to preempt McClernand's Vicksburg campaign by attempting it himself.

Grant's plan called for two separate forces to advance simultaneously and without communication, a risky proposition at best. While Grant personally led an army south along the Mississippi Central Railroad toward Jackson, hoping to draw Confederate forces out for a fight, Sherman would slip down the Mississippi River on transports and land near Chickasaw Bluffs, just north of Vicksburg. Sherman's troops then would brush aside the light Confederate opposition and seize the city. But the scheme quickly fell awry.

Two Rebel cavalry raids severed Grant's supply line, and he fell back under the misapprehension that his feint had succeeded and Sherman had captured Vicksburg. The Confederates at Vicksburg, however, did not budge from their works, and when Sherman tried to storm the bluffs in late December, Confederate shells and balls cut bluecoats down by the hundreds.

The new year brought a blend of headaches and hope for Grant and Sherman. On 2 January 1863, McClernand arrived by transport north of Vicksburg with his newly created army. Commissioned a major-general of volunteers that ranked him above Sherman, McClernand took command of all forces there. They had no prospects of capturing Vicksburg from below Chickasaw Bluffs. Sherman, therefore, proposed a joint army–navy operation against Fort Hindman, often called Arkansas Post, on the Arkansas River, from which Confederates had launched raids against Federal transit along the Mississippi River. McClernand endorsed the concept so warmly that he eventually claimed the idea as his, while Admiral David Dixon Porter needed coaxing from Sherman. Porter had all the confidence in the world in Sherman and none in McClernand, and as a result he extracted a promise from McClernand that Sherman would run the operation. On 9 January, the Federal expedition reached the vicinity of Arkansas Post, and within two days, Porter's bombardment had compelled the defenders to raise up the white flag. Nearly 5,000 prisoners fell into Union hands.

Grant, meanwhile, had resolved some important questions in his own mind about the upcoming Vicksburg campaign. Since McClernand lacked the fitness to command, he would direct operations personally. McClernand, Sherman, and a Grant protégé named James B. McPherson, a personable engineer officer who graduated first in the West Point class of 1853, would command corps.

The overland advance along the Mississippi Central Railroad had failed, so Grant explored a variety of options to get at Vicksburg. He

John A. McClernand, a politician from Illinois before the war, commanded a division at Forts Henry and Donelson and again at Shiloh. He raised troops that helped him capture Arkansas Post. McClernand commanded a corps in the Vicksburg campaign, fighting at Raymond, Champion Hill, and the assaults on Vicksburg. Quick to claim glory, he failed to gain the trust of Grant or Sherman and was removed. Later, he led a corps under Banks in the disastrous Red River campaign. (Library of Congress)

tried bypassing it, and seeking waterways that could position his army on the bluffs to the northeast of the city. 'Heretofore I have had nothing to do but fight the enemy,' a dejected Grant commented to his wife. 'This time I have to overcome obsticles to reach him.' When the last effort to turn Vicksburg on the right failed, Grant, Sherman, and Porter reconnoitered to select the best places to land troops.

But on that April Fool's Day, as he gazed across the Yazoo at the opposite slopes, he realized just how costly an attack here would be, and with no assurance of success. Lately, he had contemplated an unconventional movement that would take his army around to the enemy left flank. It was a risky proposition, but in a very different way from the frontal attack against Confederates occupying high ground. As he stood there, mulling it over in his mind, Grant determined that it was worth a try.

Grant began the campaign by asking the ever game Porter to run gunboats and barges past the Vicksburg batteries. For deception, Grant sent a cavalryman named Colonel Benjamin Grierson to launch a raid through the interior of Mississippi and come out at the Union army around Port Hudson, and he called on Sherman to feign an attack at Haines' Bluff. Meanwhile, the other two corps would march along the western side of the Mississippi River and Porter's people would shuttle them across the river to Bruinsburg, below Vicksburg. Eventually, Sherman's men would follow.

Once on the eastern side, Grant launched one of the most brilliant campaigns in American military history. By rapid marches, he continually confused his enemy. His army pounded the Confederate forces protecting Vicksburg, and then moved quickly to the northeast, where they hammered a Rebel command accumulating near the capital city of Jackson under General Joseph E. Johnston. Grant then turned back on Vicksburg, and had McClernand not attacked prematurely, he might have interposed Sherman's corps between Vicksburg and its defending columns. All told, the Union army fought five battles, and even though there were more Confederates in the campaign than Federals, Grant placed superior numbers on each battlefield and won every one of them. By mid-May, he was laying siege against Vicksburg.

The Confederate commander at Vicksburg, Pemberton, had a chance to escape. Johnston urged him to do so, but Pemberton had also received explicit instructions from President Davis to hold the city at all costs. After a council of war, Pemberton chose to hunker down and await succor from Johnston. It would never arrive.

Shortly after he besieged Vicksburg, Grant attempted to storm the Rebel works twice and was repulsed on both occasions. He also removed McClernand from command for violating a War Department directive and for general incompetence. Otherwise, he supervised a traditional siege that slowly strangled Pemberton's army. By early July, it became apparent to the Confederate general that his cause was lost. On 4 July, Pemberton

David Dixon Porter, whose father also raised David Farragut, proved to be a wonderful naval commander. Intolerant of red tape, Porter's aggressiveness and spirit of cooperation with the army won him lifetime friendship with Grant and Sherman. Porter was invaluable in the Vicksburg campaign and the fall of Fort Fisher. (Library of Congress)

taking a horseshoe-shaped position, with the ends stretching to the riverbank. On 27 May, Banks launched an uncoordinated assault. Among the participants were two black regiments, the 1st and 3rd Louisiana Native Guards. Charging well-defended fortifications, and part of the way through floodwater, the black infantrymen exhibited courage, even in the face of severe losses. The Union attack was repulsed everywhere. Again on 11 June and then 14 June, the Union columns attacked and failed. Banks resigned himself to siege, hoping to starve out the defenders. One Confederate recorded in his diary that he and his comrades ate 'all the beef – all the mules – all the Dogs – and all the Rats' they could find.

Once word of the fall of Vicksburg reached the Port Hudson defenders, Gardner knew his cause was hopeless. He surrendered on 9 July. Banks suffered 3,000 casualties in the campaign, while the Confederates lost 7,200, of whom 5,500 were taken prisoner. Lincoln could now announce proudly, 'The Father of Waters again goes unvexed to the sea.'

Crisis in Missouri

The conflict in Missouri stretched back long before the firing on Fort Sumter in April 1861. Violence first erupted in 1854 when Congress passed the Kansas–Nebraska Act, creating those territories, repealing the Missouri Compromise, which stated that all territories north of 36° 30' latitude would be free soil, and substituting popular sovereignty – a vote of the people there – to determine whether slavery could exist or not. As settlers poured into the Kansas Territory, a Northern, antislavery flavor was discernible. To tilt the balance toward slaveholders, Missourians crossed the border and cast ballots illegally and intimidated antislavery voters. Antislavery Kansans responded to violence with more violence, and soon Kansas was aflame in brutality. Border Ruffians from Missouri launched raids that resulted in rapes, murders, pillaging,

surrendered almost 30,000 Rebels and 172 artillery pieces. For the second time, Grant had captured a Confederate army.

The fall of Vicksburg left one last Confederate toehold on the Mississippi River – Port Hudson, Louisiana. Located some 25 miles (40km) north of Baton Rouge, Port Hudson consisted of extensive man-made works and natural obstructions, especially swamps. Like Vicksburg, its commander, Major-General Franklin Gardner, hailed from the North. Gardner, who had fought at Shiloh and in Bragg's Kentucky campaign, had a mere 7,000 troops to hold the position.

Against Gardner and his defenders, the Union sent Major-General Nathanial P. Banks and 20,000 troops, accompanied by Farragut's warships. From 8 to 10 May, Union gunboats shelled and ultimately silenced the batteries. Banks maneuvered his troops around the Confederate defenses, and home burning. Among those who retaliated, John Brown of Osawatomie, Kansas, led a band that savagely murdered five pro-slavery neighbors.

Strangely enough, the secession crisis of 1860–61 brought matters to a lull, as both sides struggled to size up the situation. Missouri Governor Claiborne Jackson advocated secession and called for the state to join the Confederacy. Pro-Union opposition, centered around the German-American community in St Louis and led by Francis P. Blair, a member of one of the most prominent families in Missouri, resisted. When the governor mobilized pro-secession militia and positioned them to seize the US arsenal in St Louis, Blair acted. He encouraged a fiery red-headed US army officer named Nathaniel Lyon to surround and disarm the militia, which Lyon accomplished. But as he marched his

prisoners back, a crowd of civilians gathered and harassed and abused Lyon's militiamen. Finally, someone shot and killed one of Lyon's officers, and his troops retaliated by blasting into the crowd. When the smoke cleared, 28 people lay dead.

From this moment on, the violence took on a life of its own. Union troops and opponents of slavery in Kansas and Missouri began sacking towns and seizing slaves and other property from Missourians. These acts inflamed old passions and drove many neutrals or pro-Union advocates, among them a Mexican War veteran named Sterling

John S. Pemberton (right), a Northerner by birth, commanded Confederate forces at Vicksburg. Caught between orders from President Davis and General Johnston, Pemberton could not decide whether to try to save Vicksburg or his army. He lost both. (Ann Ronan Picture Library)

Price, into the secessionist camp. After an attempt to broker a peace failed, Lyon assumed the offensive and began driving Price and pro-Confederate forces from the state. In his wake, Lyon stirred up all sorts of guerrilla bands. William Quantrill and 'Bloody Bill' Anderson led the Rebel bushwhackers. Among their followers were acclaimed robbers Frank and Jesse James and Cole and Jim Younger. From Kansas, pro-Union guerrillas included the diminutive 'Big Jim' Lane and Charles Jennison.

By August 1861, Price had accumulated 8,000 Missourians, augmented by some 5,000 Confederate soldiers under Ben McCulloch. Before he could attack, though, Lyon struck first. Unwilling to retreat and yield all the territory he had secured, Lyon elected to surprise the enemy at a place called Wilson's Creek. Initially, his attack on both flanks made headway, but a Confederate counterassault drove both back. The Rebels then focused on the Union center, where Lyon directed the fight. Although the Union commander was killed, his line repelled Price's attacks. When the smoke cleared, the Confederates had called off the fight, but the Union forces had lost 20 percent of their men and had been so badly damaged that they retreated. Price, whose command suffered slightly fewer casualties, slowly marched northward, collecting recruits and pressing all the way to Lexington, between St Louis and Kansas City.

In St Louis, the recently appointed commander of the Western Department, Major-General John C. Fremont, overreacted. The Republican Party candidate for president in 1856, Fremont declared martial law, proclaimed the death penalty for all

guerrillas, and freed all slaves of Confederate supporters. Although the emancipation directive caused outrage in the North, Lincoln privately asked Fremont to modify his order, to save the General from embarrassment. With unparalleled temerity, Fremont refused, and Lincoln had to order it.

Having irritated his commander-in-chief and many others, Fremont needed a victory to restore his reputation. He accumulated a large force, some 38,000, and began a pursuit of Price. The militia commander fell back, a good portion of his army melting back into the countryside to complete the fall harvest. An order relieving Fremont reached him before he caught up with Price.

Price's retreat into Arkansas did not quash Confederate designs on Missouri. In March 1862, Major-General Earl Van Dorn gathered 16,000 men, including some Indian troops, with Price and McCulloch as division commanders. His plan was to brush aside Union opposition and capture St Louis, a prize that would earn him accolades throughout the Confederacy. Union commander Brigadier-General Samuel Curtis, a tough old West Pointer, had other ideas. Van Dorn attempted to swing around Curtis's rear, but Yankee scouts including 'Wild' Bill Hickok spotted the movement. When the Rebels attacked at Pea Ridge, Arkansas, they made little headway. The next

Sterling Price, a Mexican War veteran and an original opponent of secession in Missouri, soured on the Union after Frank Blair and others took aggressive action to block the governor's pro-Confederate policies. He commanded Missouri's secessionist militia in 1861, led a Confederate division as a major-general at Pea Ridge in 1862, and directed the last raid into Missouri in 1864. After suffering a defeat at Westport near Kansas City, he began his retreat, enduring Union harassment along a roundabout route back to Arkansas.

day, Union artillery silenced Confederate guns, and a Federal assault swept the field.

Had the Union authorities only confronted organized armies in Missouri, they would probably have eliminated the threat in 1863. But longstanding tensions, ideological differences over slavery, and the conduct of Union troops stirred up a hornets' nest of trouble from guerrilla bands. Although many Rebel guerrillas there had strong ties to slavery, quite a few others exhibited a passion for violence and destruction that may have been pathological. Helping to ignite this tinderbox were Kansans who combined fervent abolitionism with a passion for plundering.

During the Missouri campaign of 1861, there were pockets of fighting in which neither side gave quarter. Yet raids from Kansas fueled the violence when they extended from confiscation of slaves and livestock to arson, robbery, and murder. These Kansans insisted they were merely retaliating for the slaughter of seven of their people by guerrillas a few days earlier, but acts of savagery begat more acts of savagery, and soon the entire region was ablaze in deeds of violence or brutal reprisals.

In an effort to check the acts of partisans, Union occupation troops under Major-General David Hunter and John Schofield nearly ruined their careers with repeated failures. They tried building forts in guerrilla-infested areas, but local partisans blended into the community and struck when they discovered soldiers at a disadvantage. Next, they experimented with population removal. Because guerrillas drew from friends and families for support, Brigadier-General Thomas Ewing had arrested the wives and family members of notorious guerrillas as leverage against them. Not long afterward, in August 1863, Ewing announced he would transport those under arrest as well as the families and other supporters of the Confederacy to Arkansas. Before he could do that, though, the rickety building where he housed some of the women collapsed, killing five and crippling another. Two victims were sisters of William

A West Point graduate and a former Republican congressman from Iowa, Samuel R. Curtis led a successful operation into southwest Missouri and northern Arkansas, and defeated Confederates at Pea Ridge. After heading the Departments of Missouri and Kansas, Curtis led Union forces that helped to defeat Price's Missouri Raid in 1864. (Library of Congress)

Anderson, already known for his violence. He now vowed to kill every Yankee he could find, and it was not long before he earned the nickname 'Bloody Bill.'

In retaliation, Quantrill led his party of 450 on a raid against Lawrence, Kansas, a hotbed of abolitionism. En route, they forced Kansas farmers to act as guides and then executed them. On 21 August, they slipped into town and disposed of the small number of soldiers there. The town soon surrendered, but those words meant nothing to Quantrill and his followers. All told, they murdered 150 males, wounded 30 more, and torched 185 buildings.

Federals responded to the raid by ordering all western Missourians who did not live in certain cities to migrate. Those who pledged loyalty to the Union could settle around forts, and all others would have to abandon the area. Union authorities hoped to deprive guerrillas of local support and establish free-fire zones in the area, thereby eliminating much of the worry of distinguishing friend from foe. The policy had little if any effect on the bushwhackers.

What ultimately led to the demise of guerrilla activities actually stemmed from their own success. Various partisan activities had impressed Price, particularly the work of Quantrill, and when they insisted that Missourians would rise up in support of the Confederacy if he raided into the state, Price jumped at the opportunity. With 12,000 cavalry, half of whom lacked arms, Price crossed into Missouri in mid-September 1864.

In support of the movement, various pro-Rebel bushwhackers had attacked isolated posts, towns, and pockets of soldiers, massacring troops and civilians, armed and disarmed alike. Simmering divisions began to bubble to the surface among guerrilla leaders. Anderson wanted to attack the fortified garrison at Fayette; Quantrill opposed it as too dangerous. When Anderson and his men suffered a repulse and the loss of 13 men, it only infuriated them more. A few days later, they entered Centralia in search of plunder and news of Price's whereabouts. There they pulled 25 unarmed Union soldiers off the train and executed them. When some Missouri militiamen stumbled on the guerrillas, they attacked and suffered a horrible defeat. Out of an original 147 militiamen, 129 were cut down. The guerrillas then committed a host of atrocities, including cutting off the genitals of a living soldier and placing them in his mouth.

Price, meanwhile, had advanced well into Missouri. The same day as the Centralia Massacre, his command attacked Federals under Ewing at Pilot Knob, suffering heavy losses in the repulse. As Union reinforcements arrived in Missouri, Price pressed westward along the south bank of the Missouri River. Anderson and his people met up with them, and Price sent them on a destructive spree north of the river. Before October ended, Anderson fell to two militiamen's balls. They placed his body on display, then severed his head, and eventually buried him in an unmarked grave.

As Price's columns pressed toward Kansas City, Union forces closed in on them. With Curtis to his front and Major-General Alfred Pleasanton closing from his rear, Price attempted to beat them in detail. He attacked Curtis first, and pushed the Union command back initially, but the Federals stiffened and launched their own counterattack. To the rear, Pleasonton drove back the Rebel cavalry, and Price began his retreat. Federals continued to press him, capturing 1,000 men in Kansas. Eventually, his command limped into Arkansas with only half of his original 12,000.

Price's raid was the last major Confederate undertaking west of the Mississippi River. Guerrilla fighting continued in Missouri, however, and extended well after the war, as unreconstructed bands like the Jameses and Youngers continued to rob and plunder. Quantrill, having suffered the humiliation of a rebellion in his ranks, elected to shift his base of operations to Kentucky. In May, he was shot in the back and paralyzed by Union troops. He died almost a month later.

The Tullahoma campaign

During the Vicksburg campaign, Halleck and even Grant pleaded with Rosecrans to advance. Since early in the war, the idea of liberating Unionists in East Tennessee had intrigued Lincoln. Once Grant had crossed the Mississippi River and engaged Pemberton's forces, the administration had even more reason to demand that Rosecrans attack: Union leaders feared that Bragg's army would rush reinforcements west to defeat Grant. If 'Old Rosy,' as his men called him, would advance on the Confederate Army of the Tennessee, Bragg would be compelled to hold on to all he had. In fact, Johnston did draw troops from Bragg, as well as units from the Atlantic coastal defense. Yet Rosecrans would not be rushed. Finally, after word that Union troops under Major-General Ambrose P. Burnside would push toward East Tennessee, the Union Army of the Cumberland moved out, 169 days after the Battle of Stones River.

Rosecrans may have been slow, but he was not without skills. He used a portion of his army to swing around and threaten the Confederate rear. In an effort to protect the Confederate base at Tullahoma, Bragg pulled his forces back, thereby uncovering valuable gaps in the Cumberland Plateau. With powerful Union columns pressing through them and then in on his flanks, and a raid that threatened his rear, Bragg decided to abandon Tullahoma and fall back to Chattanooga.

At comparatively little cost, Rosecrans had driven his enemy back 80 miles (129km). But he deemed further pursuit impossible. Heavy rains had impaired movements on both sides, converting roads into muck. 'Tulla,' so noted one Confederate officer, was Greek for 'mud,' and 'homa' meant 'more mud.' The halt, however, did not sit well with authorities in Washington. They could neither see rainfall nor experience the mud; all they could envision was a delay that would allow Bragg to fortify. And when Old Rosy took time to repair the railroad from Nashville, they interpreted it as his usual temporizing behavior and balked. Finally, under threat of removal, Rosecrans's army rumbled forward again in mid-August 1863, in conjunction with Burnside's advance on Knoxville.

Bragg, meanwhile, had lost the faith of his army and had begun to lose confidence in himself. His corps commanders, Polk and Lieutenant-General William J. Hardee, had voiced displeasure over his leadership. For the most part, Bragg's soldiers despised him for his strict discipline and lack of battlefield success. Under stress, especially during campaigns, he himself grew ever more despondent. Rather than view the mountains around Chattanooga as a defensive advantage, Bragg transformed them in his own mind into a Federal asset.

Because those mountains and the Tennessee River provided strong protection for Chattanooga and its defenders, Rosecrans executed a march of deception, as he had done in the Tullahoma campaign. He sent a portion of his army north of the city, to convey the impression that he was uniting with Burnside. The bulk of his army, though, crossed the Tennessee River to the southwest. By the time Bragg realized what had happened, Union forces were barreling down on his rear. On 8 September, he abandoned Chattanooga to the Federals.

To this point, in spite of delays, Rosecrans had conducted a skillful campaign. But then he got sloppy. He assumed the Rebels would fall back once again, and he divided his army for another maneuver campaign, spreading it out far too wide for the hilly terrain. Fortunately for Old Rosy, Bragg could not exploit the opportunity. Twice the Rebel commander tried to pounce on portions of Rosecrans's isolated forces, and in both instances subordinates failed to execute. In

After fighting at Iuka and Corinth, Rosecrans assumed command of the Army of the Cumberland. He led the army at the bloody engagement at Stones River. He directed the army skillfully in the Tullahoma campaign, but suffered a disaster at Chickamauga when he pulled troops from his line based on an erroneous report. Rebels attacked through the opening and routed his army. Grant replaced him with Thomas. Rosecrans finished out the war as head of the Department of Missouri. (Library of Congress)

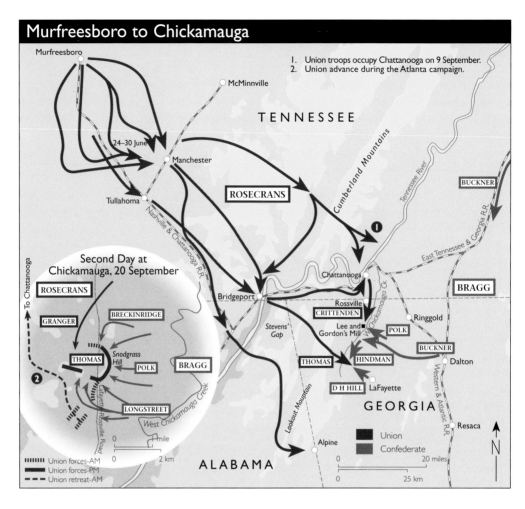

Murfreesboro to Chickamauga

1. Union troops occupy Chattanooga on 9 September.
2. Union advance during the Atlanta campaign.

haste, Rosecrans consolidated his command near a stream known as Chickamauga.

Since the spring, Confederate officials had debated the possibility of reinforcing Bragg or Pemberton from Lee's army. At the time, Lee had his own plans, a raid into Pennsylvania, and he demurred. With Bragg in need that fall, and the Union Army of the Potomac exhibiting little initiative, President Davis sent west two divisions from Lee's Army of Northern Virginia, under the command of Lee's 'Old War Horse,' Lieutenant-General James Longstreet. Traveling in a roundabout way, it took them nine days to reach Bragg's army. Major-General John Bell Hood's division arrived the day before the fight, giving Bragg numerical superiority. The next evening, Major-General Lafayette McLaws's division reached the battlefield.

On 19 September, Union and Confederate troops began to skirmish over control of a clearing. Reinforcements joined the fray piecemeal. Each time that one side extended beyond the enemy flank, a fresh batch of troops stretched beyond them. Neither Bragg nor Rosecrans could coordinate anything effective, in part because of the heavy timber around the battlefield. All they had to show for the day of fighting were lengthy casualty lists.

That night, Longstreet arrived with McLaws's division. A frustrated Bragg gave him command of the Rebel left wing and directed Polk to initiate the fight on the right the next morning. As usual, Polk made little progress, due partly to his tardiness and partly to the stout resistance of Major-General George H. Thomas's corps. In exasperation, Bragg called on Longstreet to launch an assault.

Never before on a battlefield had Longstreet fallen into such good fortune. Rosecrans had begun to pull units over to his beleaguered left, as additional support for Thomas. When a Union staff officer mistakenly reported a gap in the line on the right – the troops were actually well concealed in some woods – Old Rosy shifted some units over, this time creating a gap. Into this breach Longstreet's men fortuitously charged. Two Union divisions collapsed, racing back to Chattanooga. In their flight, they took the Union army commander with them. Once the Rebels penetrated the line, Longstreet ordered them to wheel right, to envelop the bulk of Rosecrans's command. Union units melted away, until the old stalwart, Thomas, held firm. With some timely reinforcements, the native Virginian Thomas refused to budge from Snodgrass Hill, and repeated Rebel attacks could not drive him off. At dark, he withdrew his men, earning the sobriquet 'Rock of Chickamauga' for his efforts.

In triumph, Bragg emerged in lower standing than before the battle. No one was impressed with his leadership during the course of the fight, and the bloodbath – over 18,000 casualties on the Rebels' side and more than 16,000 for the Yankees – seemed to have paralyzed him. He contributed nothing after the breakthrough, and despite pleas by Forrest and others to follow up the victory, he stalled. The Federal troops made good their escape and fortified. Eventually, Bragg took up positions to lay siege, attempting to cut off all supplies, but he lacked the resources to do so completely.

After Bragg wasted a splendid opportunity to crush the bulk of the Army of the Cumberland, old and new wounds began to fester among the Confederate high command. Bragg suspended Polk and two others for refusing to obey orders. Several generals petitioned Davis to remove Bragg, and Longstreet penned the Secretary of War, pleading with him to send Lee. Forrest rejected such niceties. He threatened Bragg to

George H. Thomas, a Virginian by birth, served as corps commander under Rosecrans. His defense at Chickamauga saved the Army of the Cumberland and earned him the nickname of the 'Rock of Chickamauga.' Appointed its commander before the Chattanooga battles, he served in the Atlanta campaign. Late in 1864, Thomas routed Hood's army at Nashville. (Library of Congress)

his face. 'I have stood your meanness as long as I intend to,' thundered the brilliant cavalryman. 'You have played the part of a damned scoundrel, and are a coward, and if you were any part of a man I would slap your jaws and force you to resent it.' Forrest then made clear that if Bragg ever interfered or crossed paths with him, 'it will be at the peril of your life.' Bragg, as well as everyone else in the army, knew Forrest would do it, too.

Finally, Davis traveled out to Chattanooga to resolve matters himself. The Rebel President relieved D. H. Hill, a good yet cantankerous officer, and transferred Polk to Mississippi. With Davis's assent, Longstreet took 15,000 men to recapture Knoxville. Yet the President failed to address the major problem, Bragg.

On the other side, Rosecrans's days were numbered. Officials in Washington tolerated his seemingly interminable delays as long as

The best cavalry commander in the Western Theater and probably on either side in the war, Nathan Bedford Forrest was a scourge to Union soldiers. Forrest's disgust for Bragg was so great after Chickamauga that he threatened to kill him. Forrest also gained notoriety when his cavalrymen slaughtered black soldiers at Fort Pillow. (Library of Congress)

he won, but after the Chickamauga débâcle they lost all faith in him. Lincoln thought Rosecrans acted 'confused and stunned like a duck hit on the head.' The Assistant Secretary of War, Charles A. Dana, visited Chattanooga and reported that the army lacked confidence in him. What the administration needed was someone to take charge. That man was Grant.

Battles around Chattanooga

Secretary of War Edwin M. Stanton caught a speedy train westward to rendezvous with Grant in Louisville. Instead, he caught up to him at Indianapolis, and the two rode together that last leg. The administration had decided to create the Military Division of the Mississippi from the Appalachians to the river, and it assigned Grant as the commander. Stanton then gave Grant a choice: he could keep Rosecrans as commander of the Army of the Cumberland, or replace him with Thomas. Grant chose Thomas.

Before Grant arrived at Chattanooga, the administration had already taken steps to improve the situation there. It had transferred the XI and XII Corps under Major-General Joseph Hooker from the idle Army of the Potomac by rail, and Sherman, with another 17,000, had been on the march from Mississippi. Rosecrans and his staff had prepared plans for opening supply lines. Grant's presence instilled confidence, and he soon had the 'cracker line' open.

With reinforcements under Sherman and Hooker there, Grant implemented his plan. Additional manpower had doubled Union

strength, while Bragg depleted the size of his command by detaching Longstreet and 15,000 men. Grant could use this considerable numerical superiority to his advantage. He ordered Hooker to attack up Lookout Mountain on the Rebel left, while Sherman's forces would roll up the right. Thomas's army, which, Grant assumed, suffered from a lack of confidence after Chickamauga, would play a less active role. It would threaten the enemy center, a long, steep hill called Missionary Ridge.

The battle opened up well for the Federals. On 23 November 1863, Thomas's people attacked and secured Orchard Knob, from which they threatened an assault on Missionary Ridge. The next day, Hooker assailed a lightly defended portion of

LEFT The Union plan did not call for Federal forces to break through the Confederate line in the center, but men from the Army of the Cumberland did just that. In the excitement of battle and their desire to restore their reputation after the disaster at Chickamauga, these Federals exploited the steep incline along Missionary Ridge, pursuing the defenders so closely that Rebels near the top could not fire for fear of hitting their own men. In a massive rush, depicted here in the sketch, Yankees carried the heights in one of the greatest assaults of the entire war. (Library of Congress)

Lookout Mountain with almost three divisions. The successful operation amid pockets of fog created quite a spectacle and gained the nickname 'The Battle Above the Clouds.' Sherman, meanwhile, had crossed the Tennessee River and planned to roll up the Rebel right at Missionary Ridge, while Hooker rushed down on the left.

Yet two factors operated against Sherman. The narrow ground and rough terrain limited his options and restricted the amount of troops he could deploy for battle. The second factor was a superb Confederate division commander named Patrick Cleburne. An Irishman by birth, Cleburne had run afoul of officials in Richmond by proposing the use of blacks as soldiers. Although he was the best division commander in the army, authorities somehow managed to overlook him for advancement, no doubt as a result of his controversial suggestion. As usual, Cleburne's

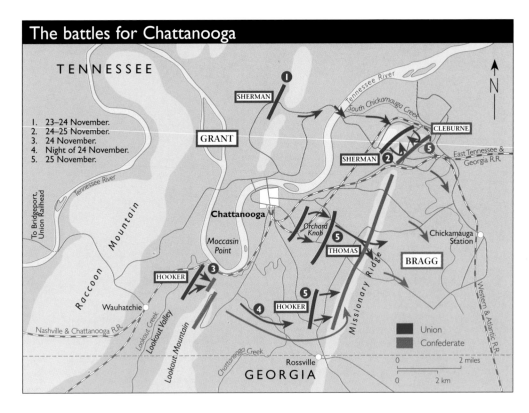

The battles for Chattanooga

TENNESSEE

1. 23–24 November.
2. 24–25 November.
3. 24 November.
4. Night of 24 November.
5. 25 November.

GRANT

SHERMAN

CLEBURNE

SHERMAN

East Tennessee & Georgia R.R.

Tennessee River

South Chickamauga Creek

To Bridgeport, Union Railhead

Tennessee River

Chattanooga

Moccasin Point

Orchard Knob

THOMAS

Chickamauga Station

BRAGG

Missionary Ridge

HOOKER

HOOKER

Raccoon Mountain

Wauhatchie

Lookout Creek

Lookout Valley

Lookout Mountain

Nashville & Chattanooga R.R.

Chattanooga Creek

Rossville

GEORGIA

Western & Atlantic R.R.

■ Union
■ Confederate

0   2 miles

0   2 km

men fought like tigers, and Sherman could make little headway against such a determined and well-led foe.

With Union plans stymied, Grant directed Thomas to order his men forward. The Union commander hoped that if men from the Army of the Cumberland seized the first row of rifle pits, it would draw Confederate reinforcements from the flanks and assist Sherman and Hooker. To the shock of both Grant and Thomas, who were standing together, soldiers in the Army of the Cumberland not only crashed through the first line of defense, they kept on going. An annoyed Grant asked who gave that order, saying there would be 'hell to pay.' Thomas admitted knowing nothing. As the defenders fell back, the Yankee troops pursued so closely that Rebels higher up the slope could not fire for fear of shooting their own men. Confederates, moreover, had chosen their primary line on the actual, not the military, crest, which created dead spaces where gunfire could not touch anyone. Federals discovered that as they clambered up the

incline, they gained these pockets of protection from enemy fire, and Rebels could not depress their artillery guns enough to hit them. On 25 November, the Army of the Cumberland exacted revenge for the Chickamauga disaster. They utterly shattered the center of Bragg's line.

Cleburne's division acted as rear guard and blocked Union pursuit. Still, Bragg had to fall back 30 miles (48km) to Dalton, Georgia, to regroup. The men in the Army of the Tennessee had no confidence in Bragg's leadership; the turmoil of high command and the detachment of Longstreet's men had caused severe damage to the morale of the men. A week after the débâcle at Chattanooga, Bragg resigned as army commander.

Nor did Longstreet's Knoxville expedition reap benefits to the Confederate cause. He advanced on Burnside, delayed, and when he did finally attack, it failed. After the rout of Bragg's army, Grant rushed Sherman with two corps to help relieve Burnside. As the Federals approached, Longstreet slipped away.

Shake-up in the high commands

Now that Chattanooga was firmly in Union hands, Grant hoped to revive plans for a major campaign against Mobile, a valuable port still under Rebel control. Instead, the administration offered a litany of missions, none of which would significantly advance the Union toward its ultimate goal of defeating the Rebels. What Grant wanted to do was launch a campaign from New Orleans to Mobile, and from there press northeast toward Atlanta, while Thomas moved from Chattanooga to Atlanta. The administration countered with a proposal that he strike into Texas.

Before they worked out their differences, though, Lincoln and Congress had concluded that the nation's most successful combat commander should direct the war effort. Congress passed legislation to create the rank of lieutenant-general, and Lincoln signed it into law. There was no disagreement over who should receive the promotion. They established the law with Grant in mind.

Major-General Joseph Hooker and his troops drove the Rebels from Lookout Mountain. Grant's plan called for Hooker to pinch the Confederates from the west, while Sherman pressured them from the east, and Thomas threatened their center. As it turned out, Hooker carried Lookout Mountain, Sherman bogged down in narrow and well-defended terrain, and Thomas's men stormed the heights of Missionary Ridge, gaining a resounding victory for the Federals. (Library of Congress)

In early March, Grant traveled to Washington to receive the promotion in person. Originally, he had intended to stay in the nation's capital briefly, just long enough to draft plans for the spring campaigns and resolve some command issues. Before he went, Sherman had advised him to return west. The politics in Washington were poison; all Grant had to do was look at Halleck to see how the pressures had affected him.

Once there, Grant soon realized that he must establish his headquarters in the east. Everyone from the politicians to the press to the public at large expected him to oversee the campaign against Lee. In their eyes, Lee's

A hero in the Mexican War, Confederate President Jefferson Davis designed a sensible strategy for the Confederacy. Unfortunately, he never found a commander in the Western Theater to match Robert E. Lee in the east. (Ann Ronan Picture Library)

army had come to symbolize the viability of the rebellion, and until Grant vanquished the Army of Northern Virginia, the revolt would continue. At the same time, Grant knew that he could not endure the endless distractions of life in the nation's capital.

As his solution, Grant formulated a novel command structure. To avoid the continual barrage of visitors and to oversee the operations of the Union forces against Lee's troops, he elected to travel alongside the Army of the Potomac. There, he could observe and, if necessary, supervise the army and its generals directly, while leaving Major-General George G. Meade in command. At the same time, he could remain relatively close to the political epicenter, Washington, DC. To handle everyday military affairs, Grant would retain former commanding general Halleck under a new title, chief of staff. A superb staff officer,

Halleck would be Grant's connection to various field commanders, summarizing their messages and relaying them to Grant for decisions and instructions. Occasionally, Halleck would issue orders or advise field commanders on his own. In the shake-up, Sherman replaced Grant as head of the Military Division of the Mississippi. Trusted subordinate McPherson took charge of the Army of the Tennessee, Sherman's old command.

The Confederates, too, underwent a command change. With Bragg's resignation, Jefferson Davis needed a new army commander, someone in whom the soldiers had faith. Hardee agreed to act as commander until the President secured someone, but he would not do it permanently. Hardee proposed Joe Johnston. Davis's old friend, Polk, also suggested Johnston, as did Robert E. Lee. Although Davis still harbored resentments for Johnston's failure in Mississippi, he had little choice. It was either him or Beauregard, and Davis opted for the lesser evil, Johnston.

Banks's Red River operation

Because of French presence in Mexico, a desire to seize valuable cotton, and a distant hope to secure complete control of Louisiana and to begin the reconstruction process, in spring 1864, Lincoln called for an expedition under Banks up the Red River. Banks would march overland to Alexandria, Louisiana, where he would link with 10,000 veterans from the Army of Tennessee under Major-General A. J. Smith, whom McPherson would loan temporarily. Their goal was Shreveport. Admiral Porter with an assortment of ironclads and gunboats accompanied Smith. In addition, Major-General Frederick Steele would march from Little Rock, Arkansas, with another 15,000. To oppose this force, the Confederates had some 15,000 men under Major-General Richard Taylor, Davis's former brother-in-law and one of Stonewall Jackson's old brigade commanders.

After a disastrous campaign in the Shenandoah valley, in which he earned the nickname of Stonewall Jackson's quartermaster, the ante bellum politician Nathaniel P. Banks took over command of the Department of the Gulf. He oversaw the fall of Port Hudson, but then led the Federal forces in the disastrous Red River campaign. Banks's late start also deprived the Army of Tennessee of 10,000 of its men for the Atlanta campaign. He was succeeded by E. R. S. Canby. (Library of Congress)

Even though Sherman instructed Banks that he must conduct the campaign promptly and return McPherson's troops for the spring offensive, Banks began late and arrived at Alexandria eight days after Smith's men had taken the town. Taylor's Confederates fell back beyond Natchitoches and halted around Mansfield, forming their defense at Sabine Crossroads. On 8 April, Federals stumbled into an unanticipated fight and suffered a rout, losing 2,500 as prisoners. Yankees fled pell mell to Pleasant Hill, where Banks prepared a defense built around Smith's corps.

The next day, Taylor attacked, and although Federals blocked the advance, Banks withdrew the next day. The Rebels pursued, harassing Banks's command and Porter's fleet at every opportunity. By the time the Yankees had reached Alexandria, low water trapped the vessels. An ingenious

engineer, Major Joseph Bailey from Wisconsin, erected a dam to build up the water level. When they broke the dam, the rushing water carried Porter's fleet to safety. Still, Confederates continued to strike at retreating Union columns until 18 May. Not only had Banks suffered a severe repulse, and nearly lost Porter's expeditionary force, but delays deprived McPherson of critical manpower in the early days of the great spring campaign. Banks's retreat allowed the Confederates to concentrate on Steele's command and defeat it as well.

Poor leadership was only part of the Federal problem, though. The Red River campaign was the product of misdirected strategy on the part of Lincoln and Halleck. They ordered the expedition over the objections of Grant and Sherman, and even Banks preferred an advance on Mobile. The administration committed (and risked) valuable resources to an enterprise that, in the final analysis, would not have brought the rebellion appreciably closer to its conclusion, even if it had been extremely successful.

The son of Zachary Taylor and Jefferson Davis's former brother-in-law, Richard Taylor led a brigade under Stonewall Jackson and was one of the few who earned his admiration. He returned west, where he served out the war. As lieutenant-general, he skillfully opposed Banks's Red River campaign and whipped the larger Union force. Taylor surrendered his command to E. R. S. Canby in May 1865. (Library of Congress)

The Red River campaign

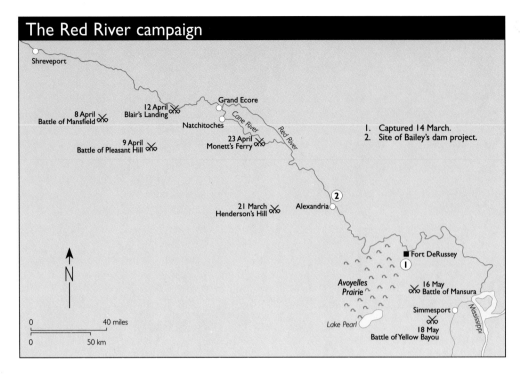

Shreveport

Grand Ecore

12 April
8 April   Blair's Landing
Battle of Mansfield

Natchitoches   Cane River

1. Captured 14 March.
2. Site of Bailey's dam project.

9 April   23 April
Battle of Pleasant Hill   Monett's Ferry   Red River

21 March   Alexandria
Henderson's Hill

(2)

Fort DeRussey

(1)

Avoyelles   16 May
Prairie   Battle of Mansura

Simmesport

Lake Pearl   18 May
Battle of Yellow Bayou

Mississippi

N

0   40 miles
0   50 km

Plans for the spring campaign

The appointment of Joe Johnston sent a
bolt of electricity through the Army of
Tennessee. After a year and a half of the
obstreperous and unsuccessful Bragg, the
men felt as if they had finally secured a real
leader. Johnston possessed an extraordinary
charisma that drew soldiers to him. Troops
felt as if he cared about them, and at least
initially, the men in the Army of Tennessee
rejoiced over his appointment. Unlike the
Commander-in-Chief, the soldiers did not
blame him for the loss of Vicksburg, and he
had the great fortune of having been
removed well before the Bragg fiasco of mid
to late 1863.

Johnston's mere presence revived the
Confederates' sinking morale, but despite
his prewar experience as the Quartermaster-
General of the US army, he could not
conjure supplies from nothing. He
addressed basic necessities like food and
clothing as well as he could, but the army
suffered from serious shortages of mules,
horses, and wagons, none of which he
could overcome.

Johnston took on the job of
commanding general with a legacy of
mistrust between him and Davis that
virtually doomed the assignment from the
start. He believed that Davis installed him
in positions that would inevitably fail,
thereby ruining the General's reputation.
Davis thought Johnston did not live up to
his potential as a military man. He was too
immersed in petty command prerogatives,
and he dabbled far too heavily in the
opposition to Jefferson Davis.

The Confederate President instructed
Johnston to communicate freely and call on
him for advice. He wanted Johnston to
produce a campaign plan, particularly one
with an offensive punch to it. Davis had
read and digested only the misleading,
positive reports of the army and convinced
himself that it should assume the offensive
that spring. Johnston kept his own counsel
and refused to provide the kind of
information his Commander-in-Chief
expected. The Army of Tennessee, moreover,
did lack the essential resources to undertake
major offensives. The best it could hope for,
Johnston believed, was to fight on the

defense, repulse a major attack by Sherman, and then counterattack.

Johnston determined to fight on the defensive around Dalton, seeking an error by the enemy to exploit. Yet in the event he had to fall back to Dalton, he failed to prepare alternate defensive positions to his rear and to design traps for Sherman's army. Throughout the campaign, when his army retreated, he and his staff had to scramble to find new defensive locations. Inevitably, he yielded the initiative and sacrificed the operational level of war for strictly tactical defensive positions.

On the Union side, upon Grant's return from Washington, he summoned Sherman from Memphis to discuss plans for the campaign season. Sherman would succeed him out west. To save time, they took the train to Cincinnati together, plotting strategy and discussing personnel changes. Two weeks later, Grant issued his plan in writing. He intended to assume the initiative on as many fronts as possible, 'to work all parts of the army together, somewhat toward a common center,' something the Union had attempted yet failed to accomplish for two years. 'You I propose to move against Johnston's army, to break it up, and to get into the interior of the enemy's country as far as you can, inflicting all the damage you can against their war resources.' Grant refused to dictate the specifics of the campaign plan; he merely requested that Sherman submit a general plan of his operations.

Rather than a single army, Sherman commanded what modern soldiers would call an army group. At his disposal for the campaign against Johnston, he had Thomas's Army of the Cumberland, McPherson's Army of the Tennessee minus A. J. Smith's people, and a small corps under Major-General John M. Schofield, head of the Department and the Army of the Ohio. Hooker remained with Sherman's forces, commanding the XI and

This map shows the movements of the combined armies of Major General William T. Sherman during the Atlanta campaign, from early May through mid-July 1864.

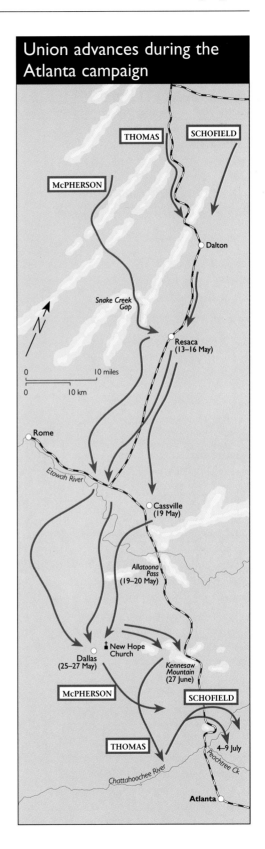

Union advances during the Atlanta campaign

Joseph E. Johnston was one of the great enigmas of the Civil War. The Confederacy expected great things from Johnston, but he never seemed to rise to meet those expectations. He fell afoul of President Jefferson Davis, who blamed Johnston for the loss of his beloved Vicksburg. Johnston returned as commander of the Army of Tennessee, only to be removed at Atlanta. (Library of Congress)

XII Corps, which he merged to form the XX Corps. Sherman's total force, infantry, cavalry, and artillery, totaled around 100,000.

Extremely sensitive to logistical issues, Sherman worried about Confederate cavalry raids striking his lengthy supply line on the campaign. He gathered large numbers of locomotives and rail cars to service his army. During the months before the campaign began, Sherman accumulated supplies and stockpiled all sorts of other necessities, such as rails, ties, and material for bridging. He directed the construction of blockhouses to protect vital positions along the rail route, and he devoted considerable numbers of troops to protecting that line of support.

After three years of active service, and years of army experience and contemplation, Sherman had concluded that the search for

the climactic battle, especially against a competent opposing commander like Johnston, was a bootless one. Large armies, sustained by industrialization, advanced agriculture, and more modern supply methods, could withstand great losses, as the Rebel Army of Tennessee and the Yankee Army of the Potomac had, and still be effective forces. Where Sherman could damage the Rebel war effort was by taking Atlanta. A manufacturing city second only to Richmond, it was also a critical rail nexus.

Originally, Sherman had planned for Thomas and Schofield to hold Johnston in place while McPherson's Army of Tennessee sliced down from northern Alabama to seize Rome, Georgia. The move might compel Johnston to fall all the way back to the Atlanta defenses. When it became clear that Banks could neither return A. J. Smith's men to McPherson nor undertake a strike on

A Grant and Sherman protégé in the war, James B. McPherson graduated first in his class at West Point. He began the war as an engineer and rose to command the Army of Tennessee. He was killed in the Battle of Atlanta. (Library of Congress)

Mobile, which would help protect the Army of Tennessee in its isolated march, and that two more of McPherson's divisions were delayed up north, Sherman had to revamp everything. Thomas, who had honed intelligence gathering to a fine art, ascertained that gaps in the mountainous country to the south and west of Johnston's army were lightly defended. Sherman determined that a bold flanking movement might be able to push into Johnston's rear, sever his rail link to Atlanta, and then strike the Rebel flank as the army retreated.

In early May, in conjunction with Grant's campaign against Lee, Sherman opened the offensive. Thomas held Johnston in place with an excellent feint, while McPherson slipped around the Rebel left flank. On 8 May, Union troops advanced into Snake Creek Gap, not far from Resaca and the railroad. But the next day, Federal troops discovered a body of Confederates in a fortified position. Uneasy over his isolated situation, McPherson decided that he lacked the strength to assail the enemy. He withdrew to the gap, but this alone forced Johnston to retreat. Had McPherson's army possessed its full complement of troops, or had Sherman accepted Thomas's offer of lending some of his army, the campaign might have proved disastrous for Johnston. As it was, the flanking movement dislodged the Rebels from a great defensive position.

As Johnston's command retreated, it picked up some valuable reinforcements. Polk brought what amounted to another corps, to join with those under Hardee and Lieutenant-General John Bell Hood, who had earned a great reputation in Lee's army as a brigade and division commander and had possessed the great fortune of spearheading the drive through Rosecrans's gap at Chickamauga.

Johnston took a defensive position around Resaca and then to the southwest along the northern bank of the Oostanaula River. After some fighting, especially on the Confederate right, Sherman's men forced a crossing over the Oostanaula, and by 15 May, Johnston had to fall back again.

The pattern of Sherman fixing and turning his enemy continued. When Johnston planned a counterstroke, as he did at Cassville, Hood hesitated. The corps commander accepted a report that Union troops were approaching his rear and canceled the attack. Johnston then fell back to the Etowah River and a formidable defensive position at Allatoona. But he could not lure Sherman into an assault. The Union command slipped again to the west, and the Rebels retreated to the area around Dallas and New Hope Church, tossing up strong field works for protection. The Federals followed suit. The two sides then skirmished with each other, but neither launched a major attack.

By shifting to the west, Sherman had drawn Johnston away from the Western & Atlantic Railroad, the Confederate supply line to Atlanta. The Union commander tried to swing his army around the Rebel right flank, gain control of the railroad, and compel the Confederates to attack him. Instead, Johnston beat him there and occupied some high ground near Marietta. In mid-June, Sherman's command butted up against the Rebels, probing for any weaknesses or opportunities. Finally, on 27 June, Sherman committed the kind of blunder that Johnston had sought weeks earlier. Believing that the Confederates had extended their line so far that it was weak in the center, Sherman hurled men up slopes in two locations. Troops in both Thomas's and McPherson's army were repulsed. At these encounters, collectively called the Battle of Kennesaw Mountain, the Union suffered 3,000 casualties, while inflicting only 600.

With Johnston and much of the Confederate army distracted by the attack around Kennesaw Mountain, Schofield's troops slid past the Rebels on the Union right and, again, Johnston had to fall back toward Atlanta, occupying a prepared line. By 5 July, McPherson had bypassed that position, and the Union flanks touched the Chattahoochee River. To get his army over the river, Sherman feigned a crossing on his right, had Thomas fix Johnston's army, and directed Schofield to cross the river

Battles around Atlanta

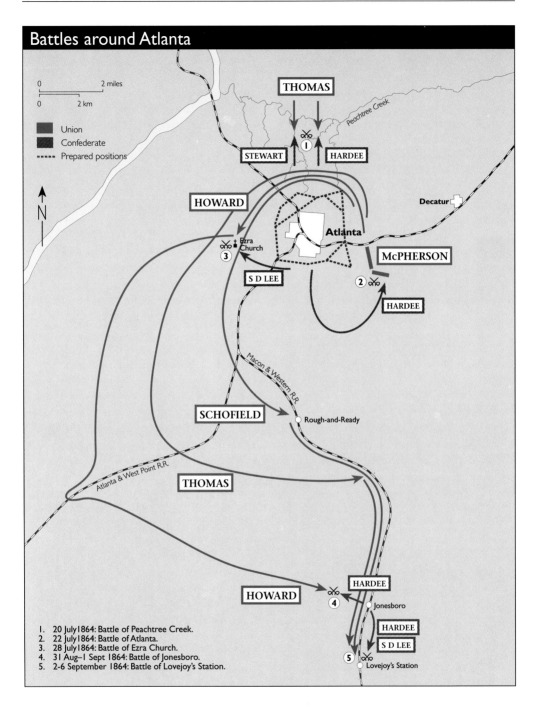

0 ————— 2 miles
0 ——— 2 km

■ Union
▦ Confederate
••••• Prepared positions

N

THOMAS

Peachtree Creek

STEWART   HARDEE

①

HOWARD

Decatur

Atlanta

Ezra Church

③

S D LEE

McPHERSON

②

HARDEE

Macon & Western R.R.

SCHOFIELD   Rough-and-Ready

Atlanta & West Point R.R.

THOMAS

HARDEE

HOWARD   ④   Jonesboro

HARDEE
S D LEE

⑤   Lovejoy's Station

1. 20 July 1864: Battle of Peachtree Creek.
2. 22 July 1864: Battle of Atlanta.
3. 28 July 1864: Battle of Ezra Church.
4. 31 Aug–1 Sept 1864: Battle of Jonesboro.
5. 2–6 September 1864: Battle of Lovejoy's Station.

upstream. As Federals worked their way over the river, Johnston had to abandon yet another powerful defensive position. He retreated to the south side of Peachtree Creek, only 3 miles (5km) from the heart of Atlanta.

As Johnston fell back closer to Atlanta, people began to lose faith in their highly touted commander. Soldiers grumbled; some cast aside their weapons and went home; still others turned themselves in to the Yankees. How far Johnston would retreat, no one knew, but soldiers and civilians alike grew more and more concerned.

LEFT

20 July, Hood executed Johnston's plan by trying to strike Thomas's army as it crossed over Peachtree Creek, using men from Stewart's and Hardee's corps. Thomas repulsed the attack.

22 July, Hood pulled Hardee's corps out of the trenches around Atlanta and sent it on a wide march around the Union flank. Scouts saw the movement, but Hardee's late arrival convinced the Federals that the movement had been canceled. McPherson's army fought off the attack. McPherson was killed in the battle.

28 July, Sherman sent Howard around to the west, to sever the railroad connections to Macon and the west. Stephen D. Lee's corps attacked him and was repulsed. When cavalry raids failed to destroy the railroads effectively, Sherman secured his hold on his supply line,

the Western & Atlantic Railroad, and shifted the bulk of his army to the south. Schofield struck the Macon & Western Railroad near Rough and Ready. Part of Thomas's army advanced about halfway between Rough and Ready and Jonesboro, and Howard's army moved on Jonesboro. On 31 August, Hardee's and Lee's corps attacked Howard and were repulsed. Lee had to withdraw, and Sherman tried to destroy Hardee's corps. He called down Thomas and part of Schofield's commands. Although the Union attacks were successful, Hardee withdrew south with most of his corps. On 2 September, men from Thomas's and Schofield's commands attacked Hardee at Lovejoy's Station. Later that day, the remainder of Hood's army arrived, and the forces skirmished for a few days before Sherman withdrew his troops to Atlanta.

ABOVE

The Western & Atlantic Railroad, which ran from Chattanooga to Atlanta, became part of Sherman's and Johnston's lifeline during the Atlanta campaign. From a

military standpoint, Allatoona Pass proved extremely important. The photograph, looking northward, demonstrates the narrowness of the area and indicates how important control of it was for both sides.

   Back in Richmond, Davis worried about the loss of Atlanta. He had received reports, including private messages from Hood, complaining that Johnston refused to fight. From the army commander himself, Davis learned little. Johnston grumbled that he lacked the manpower to assume the offensive, or that he needed additional cavalry to strike Sherman's supply line, the Western & Atlantic Railroad. In fact, the disparity between the two armies was not that severe. During Johnston's retreat, he shortened his supply line to Atlanta and picked up some additional defenders. Sherman, meanwhile, had to peel off almost 20,000 soldiers to guard his supply line.

   To get at the real situation, and to explain the issues from Richmond's perspective, Davis sent his military advisor, Bragg, to Atlanta to meet with Johnston. After speaking to subordinate commanders and Johnston over a few days, Bragg reported to the President, 'I cannot learn that he has any more plan for the future than he has had in the past.' Bragg did suspect, though, that Johnston 'is now more inclined to fight.'

enable me to anticipate events.' In reply, Johnston insisted, 'As the enemy has double our number, we must be on the defensive. My plan of operations must, therefore, depend on that of the enemy. It is mainly to watch for an opportunity to fight to advantage.' He then expressed a hope to employ the Georgia militia in the Atlanta defenses, to free up his army for movements.

That was the last straw. Davis needed to hear that he would defend the city and that he had a plan of action. Johnston offered neither. The next evening, 17 July, Davis removed Johnston and placed Hood in command.

By all accounts, Hood was an aggressive fighter. Personally courageous, he fought in the front and suffered the consequences. A ball had shattered his arm at Gettysburg, and he suffered the amputation of his leg from a wound at Chickamauga, which impaired his ability to move about and afflicted him with

The Confederacy could not afford to lose Atlanta, and Davis had to act. He needed assurance from Johnston that he would hold the city. 'I wish to hear from you as to present situation,' telegraphed Davis, 'and your plans of operation so specifically as will

John Bell Hood gained early acclaim as commander of Hood's Texas Brigade and for his breakthrough at Chickamauga. He commanded a corps throughout the Atlanta campaign, and he replaced Joe Johnston outside Atlanta. Davis assigned him to command because he would fight, and Hood did just that, but he still lost Atlanta. He was also defeated at Franklin and Nashville. (George S. Cook)

With the help of slave labor, the Confederates erected some stiff defensive works around Atlanta. The photograph, taken from the viewpoint of the Rebel cannoneers by George Barnard in 1864, shows the protection afforded them, the open terrain for effective firing, and some obstructions to impede attackers. (Library of Congress)

chronic and severe pain. He also lacked experience at high command. Yet despite his disabilities, there was no denying his aggressive spirit.

With Johnston's plan, Hood attacked Thomas's army on 20 July, as it tried to cross Peachtree Creek. Veterans in the Army of the Cumberland beat them back. He then attempted to send Hardee's corps on a lengthy march around Sherman's left to roll up the flank. Even though Federals had seen them on the march, Hardee's late attack caught them off guard. In the battle, the Yankees lost McPherson, who accidentally

John A. Logan, a former Democratic congressman from Illinois, proved to be one of the truly exceptional politician-generals of the Civil War. An excellent brigade and division commander, Logan earned the trust and respect of Grant and Sherman. The XV Corps commander, he filled in as army commander in the Battle of Atlanta when McPherson was killed. Logan commanded the XV Corps for the remainder of the war. (Library of Congress)

rode into advancing Confederates and was shot and killed. Major-General John A. Logan, probably the best of the political generals on the Union side, replaced the fallen leader and repulsed the assault. When Sherman then swung to the southeast, stretching for the Macon & Western Railroad, Hood struck once more at Ezra Church. The new commander of the Army of the Tennessee, a pious, one-armed West Pointer named Oliver Otis Howard, repelled the attack. In three battles over six days, Hood had done what Davis had asked him to do: fight. But in the process, he had suffered two and a half times as many casualties as Sherman's army, and he was in a worse position to hold on to Atlanta.

At the Battle of Atlanta, Hood attempted to roll up the Union flank. Federals observed the wide flanking movement, but Rebel delays misled Federal troops into believing that no attack would occur. Hardee's men drove the Union forces back, but Federals eventually counterattacked and held the line. Major-General James McPherson was killed while riding to the sound of gunfire, and Major-General John A. Logan oversaw the victory. (Ann Ronan Picture Library)

Sherman knew that if he could just cut the Western & Macon Railroad, Hood would be compelled to abandon the city. His cavalry failed to do the job, and he planned to pull back part of his army for defense, freeing up others for offensive operations to the southwest. Slowly, he wheeled his forces toward the railroad. In order to protect that last, vital line, Hardee launched a vicious attack against Howard's men at Jonesboro, but he could not dislodge them. With Thomas's and Schofield's columns gaining parts of the line, too, Hood had no choice but to abandon Atlanta. He exploded rail cars loaded with ammunition and evacuated his armed forces from the city. On 2 September 1864, a gleeful Sherman wired, 'Atlanta is ours, and fairly won.'

RIGHT William Tecumseh Sherman rebounded from a nervous breakdown to become Grant's most trusted subordinate. His victory in this Atlanta campaign assured Lincoln's re-election, and his revolutionary March to the Sea and through the Carolinas helped bring the war to a speedy conclusion. (Ann Ronan Picture Library)

BELOW Before Hood's army abandoned Atlanta, it destroyed an ordnance train. The explosion and fire caused massive destruction. (Library of Congress)

The presidential election of 1864

No doubt, Sherman knew just how important the fall of Atlanta was to the cause of reunion. More than a precious industrial and transportation center, Atlanta signaled the success of the commanding general, Grant, and the Commander-in-Chief, Lincoln. It could not have come at a more vital time.

Both the Union and the Confederacy understood the consequence of battlefield decisions that year. The year 1864 would see a presidential election, and by choosing Grant as his commanding general, Lincoln had linked his political future to Grant's military success. The Rebels, too, recognized its significance. If they hoped to win independence, they must extract a political decision from antiwar forces in the North at the polls. And the key to that would be military success in 1864.

The year opened with Banks's Red River fiasco, followed by stalemates in the two major campaigns. Grant incurred staggering losses in his campaigns in the east – some 60,000 casualties in seven weeks – and eventually locked into a siege with Lee around Petersburg. Sherman's columns did not suffer the same number of losses as Federals back east did, but to observers it appeared as if the Rebels under Johnston were holding their own for quite a few weeks.

More than just the antiwar supporters, more than just the loyalists of the Democratic Party, Lincoln had generated a fair amount of opposition within his own party. Conservative Republicans saw him as caving in to the Radicals, while the Radicals believed that Lincoln catered too much to the opponents of abolitionism and to those who interpreted the Constitution narrowly. Secretary of the Treasury Salmon P. Chase tested the political waters with certain elements of the Republican Party, and Major-General John C. Fremont, the party's nominee for president in 1856, openly courted support to replace Lincoln on the ticket. Both insurgencies failed, but they represented uneasiness with Lincoln's candidacy.

During the summer months, the situation grew tense for Lincoln. After the President withheld his signature and prevented the Wade–Davis Bill, a congressional plan for reconstruction, from becoming law, Wade and Davis drafted a critical manifesto that stoked the fires of opposition against Lincoln. In July, Jubal Early's raid northward nearly seized Washington. The value of Union currency plummeted. And for a while, a sullen Lincoln believed his defeat at the polls was a real possibility. He drafted a letter which he required every cabinet member to sign unseen, declaring,

This morning, as for some days past, it seems exceedingly probable that this Administration will not be re-elected. Then it will be my duty to so co-operate with the President elect, as to save the Union between the election and the inauguration; as he will have secured his election on such ground that he can not possibly save it afterwards.

But just as quickly, the tide shifted. The Wade–Davis manifesto went too far, and it pulled Republicans together, at least for the election. The Democratic Party endorsed a peace platform, and then nominated Major-General George B. McClellan, who promptly announced his continued support for the war. The fall of Atlanta sent assurances to the Northern public that the Union was going to win the war, and that Lincoln was the nation's proper steward. Then, three weeks later, a large Federal force under Major-General Philip Sheridan delivered a powerful blow against Early's raiders and followed it up with yet another.

Lincoln won re-election with overwhelming support from the army. Although not all soldiers were old enough to vote, and some states prohibited their troops in the field from participating, they rallied behind their commander-in-chief and aided his election cause any way they could. Of those who could vote, close to 80 percent cast their ballot for Lincoln, compared to 53 percent of the civilian population. In Sherman's army, about 90 percent cast their ballots for Old Abe. And whether they could vote or not, they clearly expressed their preferences to the folks at home. A Wisconsin man explained to his brother that every man who voted against Lincoln was 'a soldier's enemy.' An Illinois fellow coached his dad to 'Shun all disloyal company and do not vote the copperhead [Democratic] ticket, no matter who might say it is right.' But the bluntest talk came from an Ohioan, who instructed his sister, 'Tell Ben if he votes for Mc[Clellan] I will never speak to him again.'

Bursting with confidence after their victory at Atlanta, soldiers were assured that they would win by Lincoln's victory at the polls. 'We go with our Hartes contented,' an infantryman explained to a friend, 'nowing that we have a President that will not declare peace on no other tirmes then an Uncondishnell Surrender.'

Planning for the great march

After the fall of Atlanta, Sherman decided not to pursue Hood's army. The two forces had been in continuous contact for over 100 days, and Sherman believed his men needed a rest. He doubted that the Rebel Army of Tennessee possessed enough strength to be much of a threat to the Union cause, and he much preferred to recuperate, refit, and then undertake a very a different type of campaign from the grind toward Atlanta.

Hood's army, badly worn down but not whipped, eventually limped to Palmetto, about 25 miles (40km) from Atlanta. Morale declined over the loss of the campaign, but some rest, hot food, and time for reflection away from the boom of guns helped to restore their attitude, as did a religious revival that roared through camp. With a rejuvenated spirit, members of the Army of Tennessee began to look at the past campaign in a different light. The fall of Atlanta, concluded most of the troops, was merely a setback. Through a vast numerical superiority, the Federals had forced them out of the city, but had by no means crushed the Army of Tennessee.

During this hiatus, the Confederate President decided to pay the army a visit. Jefferson Davis had heard reports of dissatisfaction with Hood's performance throughout the Army of Tennessee and had also sensed a dramatic decline in public morale throughout the region. He hoped that a personal inspection of the army and a few public speeches on the way back to Richmond were just the solution. Upon his arrival, Davis immediately began to speak with Hood and several of his key subordinates, and it soon became clear that a major shake-up was in order. Davis promptly transferred corps commander Lieutenant-General William J. Hardee, at his own request, to the Department of South Carolina, Georgia, and Florida. Hood, however, stayed. Davis had always been fond of Hood's aggressive style, and he strongly approved Hood's new plan to strike at Sherman's long supply line and retake Atlanta. To silence critics Davis placed a more experienced officer, General P. G. T. Beauregard, in a supervisory position over Hood. Hood would still command the Army of Tennessee; Beauregard's job was merely to give Hood advice.

In addition to sorting out the command problems, Davis also hoped to give the members of the Army of Tennessee a lift. He spoke to them of the upcoming campaign and announced that they would soon advance into Tennessee and Kentucky. The President insisted that Atlanta, like Moscow for Napoleon, would be Sherman's downfall. For the most part, the Confederate troops responded favorably to Davis's predictions, yet a few of the more superstitious men feared that 'his coming is an omen of ill luck.' The last time Davis had spoken to the Army of the Tennessee was just before the catastrophe at Chattanooga.

While Major-General Joseph Wheeler and his cavalry looked after the Federals in Atlanta, Hood embarked upon a series of rapid marches along Sherman's supply line, the railroad from Atlanta to Chattanooga, destroying track and bridges and gobbling up garrisons en route. At first, Sherman jumped at the bait. He left one corps to occupy Atlanta and pursued the Confederates vigorously with the rest of his command, and on a few occasions they nearly cornered Hood's elusive army. Yet by the time the Rebels reached eastern Alabama, the Federal commander had decided to call off the hunt. It was useless for the Federals to surrender the initiative, particularly when they could not move as rapidly as the Confederates.

Since late 1862, when Grant and Sherman wrestled with guerrillas and civilian problems in Tennessee and Mississippi, they had thrashed out a strategy of raiding. Rebel cavalry had been effective against the Union army and its supply lines. Think how much disruption a Federal army could cause, the two generals speculated, if it could destroy the Confederate infrastructure, seize their slaves, damage or consume their property, and disrupt lives. The Union could demonstrate unequivocally to the Southern people just how futile continued resistance would be. In January 1864, Sherman had tested the concept in a march on Meridian, Mississippi, living off the land and wrecking anything of military value. The best thing to do, Sherman concluded, was to launch an even grander campaign. He proposed that he send a portion of his army back to Tennessee under Thomas, in case Hood pushed farther north, while he struck west for Savannah with 65,000 men.

Neither Lincoln nor Halleck liked the plan, and Grant was at best lukewarm. The commanding general much preferred that Sherman eliminate Hood's army first. But Sherman kept tossing out more and more reasons why he should go and, ultimately, he struck a responsive chord. 'Instead of being on the defensive, I would be on the offensive,' he reminded his friend, 'instead of guessing at what he means to do, he would have to guess at my plans. The difference in war is full 25 per cent.' From that moment, Grant blocked any challenges to Sherman's raid, even though he raised questions himself. Grant believed in Sherman.

For his campaign, Sherman retained four corps – the XV and XVII from the Army of Tennessee and the XIV and XX from the Army of the Cumberland – totaling about 60,000 infantry and artillery, along with a cavalry division of 5,000. These he grouped into two armies, the Army of the Tennessee under Howard and the Army of Georgia under Major-General Henry W. Slocum. To Chattanooga or Nashville under Thomas, Sherman sent back two corps, the IV and the X, plus some cavalry. Schofield elected to go with Thomas.

Even though Confederate scouts detected the passage of troops and supplies back and forth, Hood decided not to try to block Sherman's advance deeper into Georgia. The Confederate commander had come to the conclusion that he could inflict more damage on the Federal war effort by invading Tennessee and possibly Kentucky without Sherman's army hounding his rear than by chancing a battle with the larger Federal force. Although Hood still had doubts about his army defeating superior numbers in a pitched battle, he was fully confident in its ability to conduct an effective raid against the smaller Federal numbers to the north. Thus, in an anomaly of warfare, both the Federals and the Confederates terminated the campaign intentionally by marching in opposite directions from one another without having given battle.

The March to the Sea

On 12 November 1864, in preparation for the campaign, Sherman's troops began to destroy anything of military value 60 miles (96km) back from Atlanta. Some private homes along the railroad were also torched. In Atlanta, Sherman's soldiers overstepped their bounds, lighting fires throughout the town and damaging an estimated 4,000–5,000 structures. Fortunately, the population in Atlanta was light. After seizing the city, Sherman had shipped out some of the inhabitants. He saw no need to strain his food supplies for Rebel supporters.

Sherman took about 1.2 million rations with his army and a couple of weeks' worth of fodder for his animals. He had studied census records before the campaign and determined that he could supply his army from the people of Georgia, as long as his army kept moving. The key to the campaign was his reliance on the experienced nature of his soldiers. Eighty percent of his enlisted men had joined the army in 1861 or 1862. Nearly 50 percent qualified as veteran volunteers, having re-enlisted for a second term of service. They knew how to handle themselves on the march, on the battlefield, and in camp. To feed his army, Sherman would have to disperse foragers into the countryside, often with loose supervision, and here that experience proved critical.

Against his army of 65,000, for much of the campaign the Confederates could only muster Major-General Joseph Wheeler and his 3,500 cavalrymen and some militia. On the march, Sherman intended to interpose his army between two valuable military targets. The Confederates could either protect one or divide their forces, weakening resistance more. Thus, Sherman positioned his army between Macon and Augusta, two valuable industrial sites. Sherman realized

Before Sherman's army abandoned Atlanta, it destroyed the railroads. Groups of soldiers picked up rails and dislodged the ties. They then started large fires with the ties and laid the rails over them. Once the rails got red hot, men twisted the rails. Since the Confederacy had no other foundries outside Richmond that could produce rails, Sherman's men did not have to undertake the backbreaking work of filling in the rail gradings. They employed this technique through the Savannah and Carolinas campaigns, destroying 443 miles (713km) of railroad. (Library of Congress)

that he did not have to capture those cities, which could prove costly and tie down his army. All he had to do was destroy Confederate facilities for moving their products, specifically the railroads, to accomplish his goal.

Sherman's army swung down as if to threaten Macon, home of an arsenal, armory, and laboratory, and then shifted up toward Augusta, which housed the great Arsenal and Gunpowder Works and the Naval Ordnance Works. Meanwhile, his army ripped up railroad track, burning ties and twisting rails. They did not have to waste time filling in the rail grade, because if his men did their work properly and twisted the rails (sometimes, they only bent them), the Confederacy had no facilities outside Richmond to melt down and roll rails. As Sherman advanced toward Augusta, he again maneuvered his army between Augusta and Savannah, confusing the Confederates as to his real destination and enabling his men to do their work. On the Savannah campaign, Sherman's troops destroyed over 300 miles (480km) of rail.

The campaign caused quite a sensation among people North and South. Few knew Sherman's true destination, Savannah, and the way he cut a swath right through the state of Georgia fascinated Northerners and terrified Southerners. By marching through the countryside, Sherman's soldiers frightened the people of Georgia. Hordes of bluecoats poured over farms, plantations, and towns, stripping the area of foodstuffs, livestock, and able-bodied male slaves, and destroying any items of military value they could not carry. Confederate soldiers in distant armies grew extremely uneasy over the welfare of loved ones and their life's work. Just as Sherman made Confederate commanders in Georgia choose between Macon and Augusta, so he forced Georgia soldiers to decide whether their ultimate responsibility lay with their beleaguered families or with the army. Before the campaign, he had vowed, 'I can make the march, and make Georgia howl.' And he did.

By the second week of December, Sherman's columns were approaching the area around Savannah. Grant had notified the Union navy of Sherman's intention, but no one knew for sure when he would surface. To open communications, Sherman's troops stormed Fort McAllister south of the city, and then stretched out to trap the garrison in Savannah. Some 13,000 Confederates under Hardee defended the city and were able to keep open one route of escape. On the night of 21 December, Hardee withdrew before Sherman could complete plans to box the Rebels inside the city. The next day, Sherman announced to the President, 'I beg to present you, as a Christmas gift, the City of Savannah.' In reply, Lincoln admitted his uneasiness over the operation and acquiesced only because 'you were the better judge' and 'nothing risked, nothing gained.' The President then insisted, 'the honor is all yours.'

Hood's Tennessee campaign

Although Hood had lost Atlanta, Confederate President Davis retained his faith in him. Davis had appointed Hood because he was a fighter, and that was exactly what Hood did. Yet the Rebel President detected a lack of seasoning in high command, and to assist Hood, Davis assigned Beauregard as commander of the Military Division of the West. Beauregard had restored his reputation somewhat with Davis by performing well as commander of the Department of South Carolina, Georgia, and Florida, and then around Petersburg. Davis did not intend for Beauregard to supersede Hood. Rather, he wanted Hood in command, but felt that Beauregard could help shape Hood's plans and provide the kind of advice that the young, aggressive warrior needed.

Hood convinced himself that he had achieved a great success by striking Sherman's supply line, and now he planned to invade Tennessee and perhaps Kentucky. If Sherman pursued, he could give battle on his own terms. If Sherman refused to follow his army, then Middle Tennessee and perhaps more would be easy pickings. Beauregard weighed in by sending Forrest's cavalry to cooperate with Hood's army and by shifting the Rebel supply base to Tuscumbia, Alabama, on the Memphis & Charleston Railroad. Beauregard then offered some advice on how to conduct the campaign: to succeed, Hood must move rapidly.

Instead, Hood dawdled. He wasted time trying to capture a Federal garrison at Decatur, Alabama, and struggled to find an acceptable crossing at the Tennessee River. Finally, he marched to Tuscumbia and waited for fresh supplies before entering Tennessee. This indecisiveness, so uncharacteristic of the impulsive Hood, may have been purposeful. Had the Rebel army advanced into Middle Tennessee along the railroad to Nashville, Sherman might have pursued, blocking Hood's escape route southward. By shifting his army to north central Alabama, Hood discouraged Sherman from chasing him.

On the Union side, Hood's movements may have baffled Sherman temporarily, but Grant assessed the Confederate commander's intentions exactly. Once the Army of

Tennessee marched to Tuscumbia, Grant realized that any pursuit by Sherman made no sense. His trusted lieutenant must strike out for the coast with the bulk of his army, yet return enough men to Nashville for Thomas to defend Middle Tennessee.

A large part of Thomas's command came from Sherman's army during the Atlanta campaign. Major-General James Harrison Wilson took back 12,000 unmounted cavalrymen, armed with seven-shot Spencer repeating carbines, and began combing the region for fresh horses and equipment. Schofield's X Corps and the IV Corps under Major-General David Stanley gathered around Pulaski, Tennessee, to check a northward advance. Grant directed A. J. Smith's two divisions of 10,000 veterans, fresh from the defeat of Price, to move by rail from Missouri to Nashville, and

Major-General James B. Steedman brought back 5,200 men from occupation duty along Sherman's old railroad supply line. In Nashville itself, Thomas had some post guards, quartermaster troops, and 14 artillery batteries to supplement the command.

Finally, on 19 November 1864, Forrest's cavalry led Hood's advance, followed by the three corps. Scouts estimated Schofield's forces at around 15,000. With about 30,000 infantry and artillery and 5,500 horsemen, Hood hoped to push north rapidly, slip around the Federal force, and seize Columbia, compelling Schofield to fight his way to Nashville. Despite nasty weather and deep mud, the Confederates made good progress. After some initial hesitation, Schofield detected Hood's plan and narrowly beat Forrest's cavalrymen back to Columbia. The Yankees occupied some

The Savannah campaign

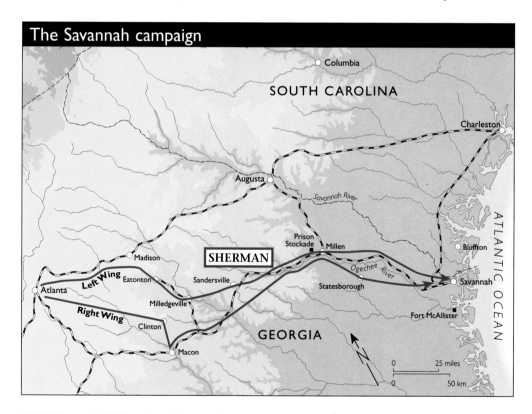

ABOVE Sherman's Left Wing advanced up toward Madison and swung down through Eatonton and into Milledgeville. From there, they pushed on through Sandersonville, Millen, and into Savannah. Sherman's Extreme Right Wing dipped down via

McDonough and through Jackson and Clinton to just north of Macon. They then struck out for Savannah by way of Millen and Statesborough. Once William Hazen's Division stormed Fort McAllister on 13 December, Sherman had a secure communication line to the US Navy.

The sketch is by Theodore R. Davis, an eyewitness of Brigadier-General William B. Hazen's division of the XV Corps storming Fort McAllister, near Savannah, Georgia. Sherman needed Hazen to seize Fort McAllister in order to open supply lines with the Union navy. Hazen used sharpshooters to pin down the defenders, and he assembled his men in a relatively thin line to reduce casualties. In 13 minutes, Hazen's troops captured the fort, with a loss of 24 killed and 110 wounded, mostly from land mines. His men inflicted 250 casualties. The sketch appeared in *Harper's Weekly*, 14 January 1865.

prepared trenches on the south side of Duck River. Several days later, as the great Rebel horseman began to force river crossings, Schofield fell back once again.

Schofield did not believe that Hood could move his army along a roundabout and difficult course and still beat him to Spring Hill. He was wrong. Confederate cavalry and then some infantry arrived before many of Schofield's troops, yet they could not check the Union retreat. Stanley had rushed a division back in the afternoon and a second one around sunset. With the aid of some artillery, these Yankee troops repelled piecemeal Rebel attacks. That night, miscommunication among the Rebel high command and a string of unfortunate decisions enabled Schofield to march

The author of an infantry tactics manual and a corps commander in the Army of Tennessee, William J. Hardee turned down command of the army after Missionary Ridge. He served under Johnston and Hood in the Atlanta campaign, and was transferred at his own request to the coastal defense, where he opposed Sherman's army at Savannah. Hardee also fought at Averasborough and Bentonville. (Library of Congress)

unhindered right past the Confederate forces and through Spring Hill. By morning, weary Federals had stumbled into Franklin, on the south side of the Harpeth River, 18 miles (29km) from Nashville. Immediately, officers put them to work fortifying some old, overgrown trenches, while engineers built two pontoon bridges across the river.

When Hood realized that the Yankees had escaped, he seethed with anger. Everyone was to blame except, of course, himself. Hood had long believed that entrenchments stripped soldiers of their aggressiveness, and he determined to teach the officers and men of the Army of Tennessee a lesson. The Rebels pursued rapidly, and when they came upon Schofield's troops at Franklin in the mid-afternoon, Hood ordered them to storm the works.

The relatively open, gently inclined terrain offered the Yankees an excellent line of fire. Still, Hood's men struck, and did so with fury. In the center of the Federal fortifications, where the Union maintained an advanced post, Rebels penetrated by following on the heels of those in flight. A vicious counterattack restored the line. Elsewhere, despite extraordinary bravery on the part of thousands of Confederates, Schofield's men repulsed the assaults.

On the last day of November, in less than three hours, Hood's army suffered almost 5,500 casualties. It was not a matter of courage; these Rebels exhibited plenty of that. The fact was that, in most instances, attackers were no match for veteran defenders fighting from behind breastworks, well armed with rifled muskets and supported by artillery. When the Union retreated to Nashville that evening, they took with them 702 prisoners, most of them captured as Federal troops sealed the penetration. The Yankees suffered 2,326 casualties.

At Franklin, Confederate commanders fought from the front and suffered staggering losses as a result. Twelve generals went down, six of them killed, and 54 regimental commanders fell in the fighting that day. Among those who lost their lives was Patrick Cleburne, the great Confederate division commander.

The next morning, Hood's soldiers marched past the grisly sight of the previous day's débâcle, crossed over the Harpeth, and began a slow advance up near the Union defenses of Nashville. At the time, Hood assumed that Thomas had not received substantial reinforcements, but he also believed that the Battle of Franklin had cut any offensive inclinations out of his army. Lacking the strength to lay siege to the city, he stretched his army out to cover the major roads heading southward and hoped that his presence might induce Thomas to attack him. A few days later, Hood detached some infantry and cavalry under Forrest to harass a Union garrison at Murfreesboro. It was Hood's hope that fear of losing those troops might induce Thomas to abandon his works and attack the Rebels.

Back in Nashville, Thomas had worried that he might not have enough soldiers to cope with Hood's army. But on 1 December, as Schofield's columns entered the city, A. J. Smith's and Steedman's troops arrived as well. Now all Thomas needed was enough good mounts and saddles so that Wilson's cavalry could compete with Forrest's vaunted horsemen and some good fighting weather. Yet just before Wilson accumulated enough horses and equipment, snow and sleet descended on Middle Tennessee, and for five days it scarcely let up. A thick sheet of ice blanketed the ground, making it nearly impossible for land movement by man or beast.

Meanwhile, Grant and officials in Washington had become increasingly uneasy over Thomas's delay. By the Union commanding general's calculation, Hood possessed fewer than 30,000 infantry and artillery, and while he thought it was possible that Forrest had more cavalry, Wilson's men carried repeating carbines which gave them an incredible firepower advantage. At one point, Grant nearly removed Thomas. He feared Hood would swing around Nashville and raid northward, wreaking havoc wherever he went. Only when Halleck balked did Grant yield. After Grant implored him to attack, Thomas declined. The ice storm prevented

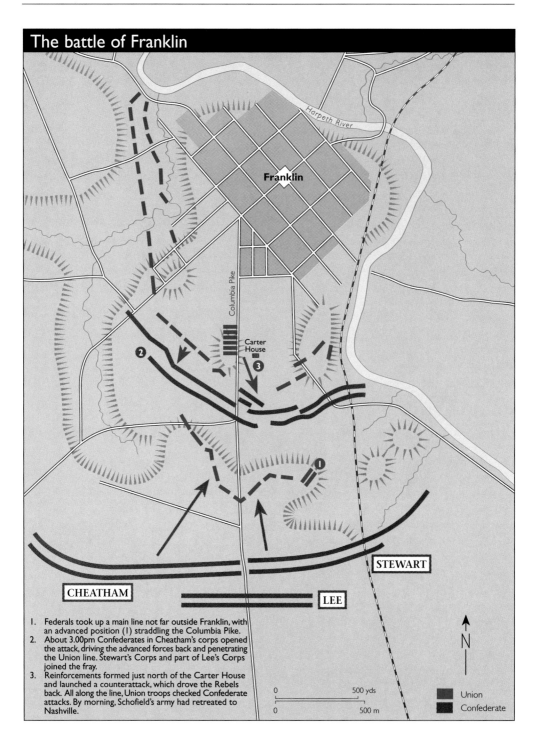

The battle of Franklin

Harpeth River

Franklin

Columbia Pike

Carter
House

STEWART

CHEATHAM

LEE

1. Federals took up a main line not far outside Franklin, with
    an advanced position (1) straddling the Columbia Pike.
2. About 3.00pm Confederates in Cheatham's corps opened
    the attack, driving the advanced forces back and penetrating
    the Union line. Stewart's Corps and part of Lee's Corps
    joined the fray.
3. Reinforcements formed just north of the Carter House
    and launched a counterattack, which drove the Rebels
    back. All along the line, Union troops checked Confederate
    attacks. By morning, Schofield's army had retreated to
    Nashville.

N

| 0 | 500 yds |
| 0 | 500 m |

■ Union
■ Confederate

movement. Once it melted, Old Pap vowed
to attack immediately.

For a few days, Grant accepted the
explanation, but impatience got the best
of him. He ordered Major-General

John A. Logan to travel to Nashville and
take over from Thomas, and after some
consideration, Grant decided to go himself.
As Grant waited to board a train in
Washington, word arrived that Thomas

The battle of Nashville

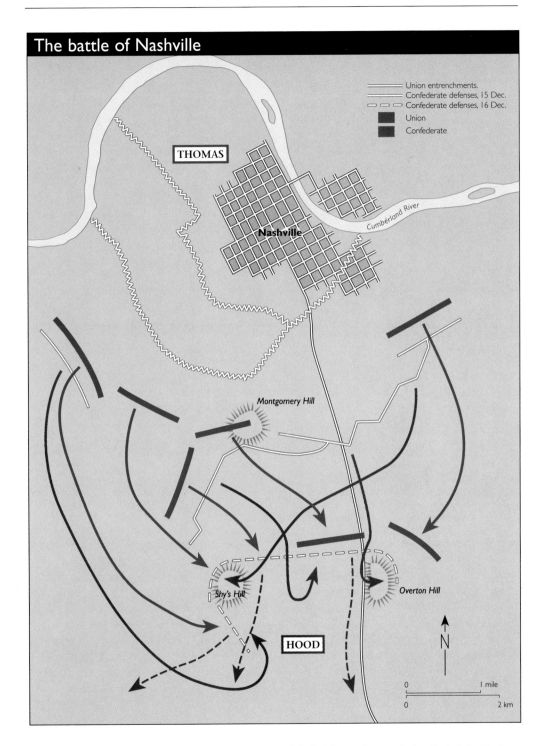

Union entrenchments.
Confederate defenses, 15 Dec.
Confederate defenses, 16 Dec.
Union
Confederate

THOMAS

Cumberland River

Nashville

Montgomery Hill

Shy's Hill

Overton Hill

HOOD

N

0 — 1 mile
0 — 2 km

had attacked and won. Grant traveled no farther.

On 15 December, Thomas launched a massive and extremely successful attack. His plan called for the Union to feint on the Rebel right and overwhelm their left. Under a cloud of fog, Steedmen's black soldiers delivered a powerful blow on the Confederate right that distracted them. On the opposite flank, A. J. Smith's troops and

ABOVE After some difficult service in Missouri, John M. Schofield served as head of the Department of the Ohio. He commanded the X Corps in Sherman's army in the Atlanta campaign. At Franklin, he repulsed a vicious Confederate assault, and his men proved critical in the flank attack at Nashville on the first day. Late in the war, Schofield commanded the expedition that seized Wilmington, and at Goldsboro his command of 40,000 united with Sherman for the final push against Johnston. (Library of Congress)

RIGHT This is a sketch by artist William Ward, who accompanied Sherman's army, of part of Logan's XV Corps as it waded across the Little Salkahatchie River in South Carolina in February 1865. Sherman's soldiers endured considerable hardships, like wading a swamp and a river in wintertime, during the Carolinas campaign. The sketch was published in *Harper's Weekly*, 8 April 1865. (Author's collection)

Wilson's cavalry crushed or completely bypassed the Rebel left. Then, late in the afternoon, Thomas hurled Schofield's men into the fight, and a massive Union assault compelled Hood's army to abandon the field.

The Rebels fell back to a new, more defensible position, but when Thomas attacked the next afternoon, the results proved even more disastrous for Hood. Once again, Thomas struck the Rebel right first, and with Rebel attention riveted there, Union infantry and cavalry swamped the left. As Federal infantry and dismounted horsemen penetrated into Hood's rear, the Rebel line crumbled, and the rout was on. Thousands of Johnny Rebs surrendered. One Confederate described the

flight as a 'stampede' and 'a sad, shocking sight to behold.' Unlike the last Confederate disaster, Wilson ordered his men back to get their mounts, and the Yankees, both cavalry and infantry, pursued with vigor.

During the two-day battle, Thomas's men took nearly 4,500 prisoners, including four generals. Wilson's pursuit snared another 3,200, of whom nearly 2,000 were wounded men at Franklin. Through Christmas Day 1864, Federal cavalry pressed the retreating Confederates. Not until Rebels crossed the Tennessee River, and Forrest assumed command of the rear guard, did Wilson ease up. Union infantry kept pace for a while, but by 22 December, Thomas had directed them

to proceed at a more leisurely speed and root out Rebel stragglers. For the campaign, Thomas's army took 8,635 prisoners and 320 Confederate deserters. As the attacking force, the Federals lost 3,061 and killed or wounded about 1,800 Rebels.

Thomas's campaign broke the back of the Army of Tennessee. While some of its members would fight again, and fight well, it no longer existed as an army in the true sense. The resounding Union victories at Franklin and Nashville, moreover, added great luster to Sherman's March to the Sea. Only such a resounding triumph would vindicate Sherman's decision to send back two corps and cavalrymen

and head to the coast on his raiding strategy.

Campaign through the Carolinas

When Sherman arrived safely in Savannah, in December 1864, Grant had great plans to transport his army by water to the Petersburg area. With the addition of 65,000 veterans, the Federals could easily stretch around Lee's flanks and bring an end to the war in the east. But Sherman had other ideas. He hated the prospect of shipping his troops by water. Would it not be better, he proposed, to march his army through the Carolinas to Virginia, destroying railroads and anything of military value en route, as he had done in Georgia? Once Grant learned that it would take weeks and weeks to assemble enough transport ships, he authorized the Carolinas campaign.

Like their commander, Sherman's soldiers much preferred to march to Virginia by way of South Carolina. They viewed that state as the hotbed of the secession movement and blamed its people for all the lives lost, bodies maimed, and hardships endured. They were almost giddy at the prospect of exacting vengeance for instigating the war.

By comparison with the advance on Savannah, the Carolinas campaign was far more difficult. Federal troops had to march through swampy country in wintertime, often amid heavy rains. Because of the terrain, South Carolina lacked the bountiful food harvests of central Georgia. And as the Federals entered North Carolina, the Confederacy had assembled a sizable force to contest the advance, which in the previous campaign occurred only as Sherman's troops approached Savannah.

Once again, Sherman used two prized targets to confuse Rebel resistance about his initial destination. Two corps appeared as if they were marching on Charleston, while the other two threatened Augusta. Instead, Sherman employed the XV and XVII Corps to uncover the route for the XIV and XX more inland. Then, his army, often taking separate roads, advanced toward Columbia. As they destroyed railroads along the way, they isolated Charleston and compelled its abandonment.

These Yankee veterans were intent on punishing South Carolina. When a soldier in the XIV Corps crossed over the bridge into the state, he yelled back, 'Boys, this is old South Carolina, let's give her hell,' at which his comrades cheered. Without authorization, they burned parts or most of 18 towns and plundered or wrecked all sorts of private property. Sherman's troops would have their revenge.

After some skirmishing, the army entered Columbia, where the troops discovered that Confederates and civilians had begun looting shops and had left stacked bales of

cotton on fire. That night, the wind kicked up and revived the flames, floating these burning projectiles to nearby buildings. In their revelry, Sherman's soldiers actively spread the fires. By morning, after the winds had died down, military officials had restored some order. One-third of the city lay in ashes. Yet Sherman's troops had not had their fill. They torched parts of five more towns in South Carolina.

Once the army crossed over into North Carolina, officers issued orders to remind the soldiers that North Carolina had been the last state to secede and had a strong Unionist minority. They urged troops to distinguish between the people of the Tarheel State and South Carolina. The army destroyed the arsenal in Fayetteville, and some firebugs burned several blocks. Generally, though, Sherman's men behaved themselves much better in North Carolina. In an army of 65,000, men plundered, especially soldiers who acted as foragers, but most soldiers eased up on their destructiveness.

By the time Sherman's troops reached North Carolina, the Confederates had begun to accumulate some forces to resist the advance. South Carolinian Lieutenant-General Wade Hampton brought cavalry from Lee's army and superseded Wheeler. Remnants of Hood's Army of Tennessee augmented Hardee's command that escaped from Savannah, and as the army fell back, they collected various coastal garrisons. On the advice of Lee, Davis restored Joe Johnston to command them all.

Despite Johnston's weakness in manpower, he had to try to block Sherman's movements. Implementing a plan devised by

RIGHT Sherman sent the XVII and most of the XV Corps by water through Beaufort. As they advanced inland, they uncovered the route for the other troops. The Right Wing (XV and XVII Corps) traveled through Orangeburg, Columbia, Cheraw, and then on to Fayetteville, North Carolina. The Left Wing passed west of Columbia through Winnesboro and then on to Fayetteville. From there, they moved on to Goldsboro, fighting at Averasborough and Bentonville. At Goldsboro, they rendezvoused with Schofield and 40,000 men from Wilmington. Joseph E. Johnston surrendered his forces near Durham.

The Carolinas campaign

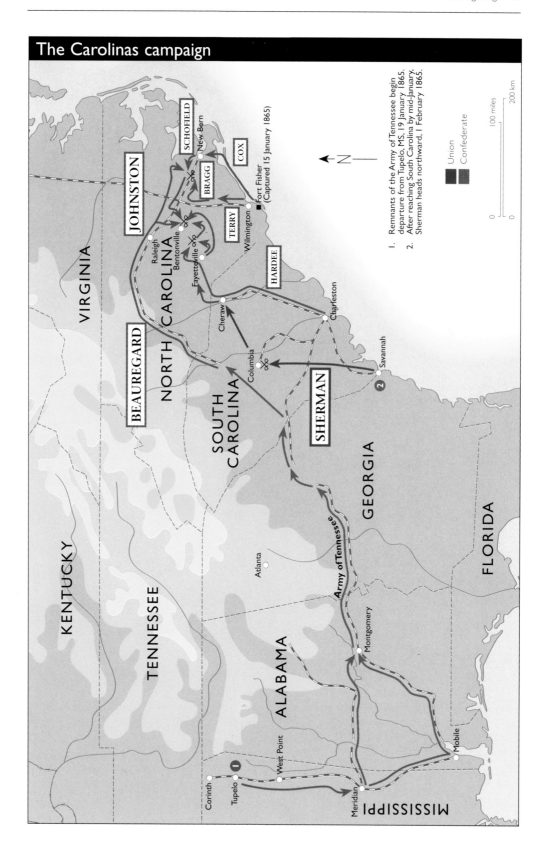

VIRGINIA

NORTH CAROLINA

SOUTH CAROLINA

KENTUCKY

TENNESSEE

ALABAMA

GEORGIA

FLORIDA

MISSISSIPPI

SCHOFIELD

COX

BRAGG

JOHNSTON

TERRY

HARDEE

BEAUREGARD

SHERMAN

JOHNSTON

New Bern

Fort Fisher
(Captured 15 January 1865)

Wilmington

Raleigh

Bentonville

Fayetteville

Cheraw

Charleston

Columbia

Savannah

Atlanta

Montgomery

Mobile

Meridian

West Point

Tupelo

Corinth

Army of Tennessee

1. Remnants of the Army of Tennessee begin
    departure from Tupelo, MS, 19 January 1865.
2. After reaching South Carolina by mid-January,
    Sherman heads northward, 1 February 1865.

N

Union
Confederate

0   100 miles
0   200 km

This sketch, prepared by an eyewitness and published in *Harper's Weekly*, 1 April 1865, shows men in the XIV Corps crossing the Catawba River at Rock Hill, South Carolina, on a pontoon bridge in the rain. That February it rained heavily in South Carolina, increasing water levels in rivers and making river crossings much more dangerous. Sherman's engineers and pontooneers were experts at laying bridges. (Author's collection)

Hampton, he directed Hardee to delay the advance by fighting at Averasborough, which he did successfully on 16 March 1865, at a loss of 800 men. This bought more time to accumulate additional troops and set the trap. Hampton devised a fishhook-shaped position, and some Federals walked right into it. On the morning of 19 March, when

Rebels and threatened their rear, until Sherman recalled the troops. Sherman was convinced that the end was near, and he loathed the idea of spilling any more blood. The Battle of Bentonville ended, with Johnston losing 2,606 men in the attack and Sherman suffering 1,527 casualties.

Three days later, Sherman marched into Goldsboro, North Carolina, where his troops closed the campaign. His army had marched 470 miles (756km), destroyed hundreds of miles of rail, wrecked an arsenal, burnt towns, and terrified civilians along the route. Yet like the Savannah Campaign, impact of the march through the Carolinas extended far beyond those who experienced it. Even Southerners who avoided the destruction suddenly confronted the reality that the Confederacy could no longer protect its citizenry. In effect, Southerners were at the mercy of Yankee hordes. By destroying railroads, Sherman's army impaired the ability of Robert E. Lee to draw supplies to Richmond, inflicting greater hardship on those beleaguered Confederates. The disruption of communication caused widespread anxiety about loved ones in those regions. And perhaps most importantly, Sherman's march encouraged massive desertion from Confederate armies by forcing Rebel soldiers to choose their ultimate responsibility, between their country and their family. When Confederate troops learned how their loved ones were suffering, many veterans deserted the ranks to care for them, and quite a number of their officers could not blame them. The problem reached such epidemic proportions in the Rebel army of Northern Virginia that Lee himself wrote the governor of North Carolina, alerting him that letters from home were promoting desertion and imploring him to rally the people of the Tarheel State to support the Rebel cause. In the end, neither the governor nor Lee could stem the tide of desertion. More than a campaign against an army, Sherman targeted a hostile people. Through his destructive marches, he shattered Confederate resolve to continue the rebellion.

some bluecoats reported resistance, Sherman brushed it aside as nothing more than cavalry in their front. Suddenly, Confederates sprung the trap and rocked back the advancing Federals, but as additional Union units rushed to the sound of gunfire, the Yankees stiffened. Two days later, a Union counterattack cut through the

The Battle of Fort Fisher and the arrival of Schofield's command

En route through South Carolina, Sherman's army sought revenge against the hotbed of secession, the state that, in their opinion, initiated this unnecessary war. Here, sketch artist William Waud, an eyewitness, depicted the burning of McPhersonville, South Carolina. Sherman's troops burned part of 18 different towns in South Carolina. (Author's collection)

Although the Union blockade had reduced much of the traffic flow on the high seas, the Confederacy continued to bring in goods and military supplies through Wilmington, North Carolina. A massive Rebel bastion called Fort Fisher protected the mouth of the Cape Fear River, with Wilmington just 20 miles (32km) upriver. After the débâcle on the Red River, Admiral Porter, the new commander of a flying squadron on the Atlantic, suggested to his old friend Grant a joint expedition to knock Fort Fisher and Wilmington out of the war. Grant assigned Major-General Godfrey Weitzel, a clever engineer, to work with Porter, but Fort Fisher was part of Major-General Benjamin Butler's department, and Butler took over direction of the project. Butler proposed a scheme to explode a ship loaded with gunpowder under the fort, which he thought would demolish it. When the ship explosion failed to damage the fort, Butler sent only 2,500 men ashore and then canceled the attack.

As Porter fumed, Grant dispatched a more capable officer, Major-General Alfred Terry, and an additional brigade. Porter and Terry cooperated brilliantly. After heavy naval gunfire softened the defenses, Terry's troops and 1,000 sailors and marines landed on the beach. The next day, 14 January 1865, again under cover from naval gunfire, Terry's men stormed the timber and sand bastion. By nightfall, Fort Fisher had fallen into Union hands.

To assist Sherman and secure the fall of Wilmington, Grant pulled Schofield and his XXIII Corps from Thomas's army and injected them into North Carolina with Terry's men. The combined force captured Wilmington, and in late March, Schofield rendezvoused with Sherman's army at Goldsboro, North Carolina, bringing 40,000 troops and ready access to some much-needed supplies.

Black soldiers and POWs

'For a man to enjoy the service, he must not be averse to much strong drink, must not be encumbered with morals & must possess an insatiable appetite for confusion,' quipped a Minnesotan. The soldier was one among some three million who responded to the call of their governments. Almost all of them volunteers, they entered military service wide-eyed, anticipating glory and rapid success. Instead, they experienced a world of hardship, heartache, and frustration.

Like the America from which they came, most Civil War soldiers were from farming or rural backgrounds. These men were an industrious, self-reliant lot, an unusual blend of idealism, individualism, and practicality. They depended on their own labor and judgment for survival, which fostered confidence in their decision-making ability. Accustomed to forming their own opinion about matters, and resistant to regimentation from the outside, their sense of independence proved both the boon and bane of their military existence.

While all sorts of pressures – family, friends, community, perceptions of manhood, quests for glory – worked on them, in the end it was that ability to decide for themselves that led most to enlist. Southerners entered military service to protect hearth and home and to defend their 'rights' – to own slaves, to take those slaves wherever they saw fit, and to live without fear of others encouraging servile insurrection. Since the US government seemed opposed to protecting those rights, they seceded and formed a new government, one that would protect them. Yankees, by contrast, believed in the permanence of the Union. Barely 80 years old, the United States was the great experiment in a democratic republic. 'It was,' so argued an Indiana sergeant, 'the beacon of light of liberty & freedom to the human race.' Secession trampled on an inherent principle of any democratic government that all would abide by the outcome of a fair election. They went off to war to sustain that government and the underlying concept because, one Yankee reasoned, 'constitutional liberty cannot survive the loss of unity in the government.' Only a minority early in the war fought for abolitionism. Although many Northerners disliked slavery, most also believed that African-Americans were inferior beings.

In 1861, soldiers rushed off to war amid celebrations and cheers. Believing the war would be short, most had the misplaced fear that the fighting would end before they saw any action. Few of them anticipated just how difficult prolonged military service would be, and how demanding life in uniform could be. Most soldiers did not know how to cook or care for themselves in camp and on the march. They loaded themselves down with excess baggage, never realizing how burdensome it was on a 15 or 20 mile (24–32km) hike. Then, when winter rolled around, they shivered through cold days and nights, cursing that Indian summer day when they had discarded their overcoats. Rather than enemy bullets, they succumbed to diseases in staggering numbers. Childhood illnesses had seldom afflicted people in rural communities, but once they gathered in large armies, these pathogens spread throughout camps, and farm boys had no resistance to them. Failure to enforce proper sanitary practices took unanticipated tolls, as camps bred pestilence and promoted the transmission of diseases at epidemic rates. As one Iowan wryly concluded, 'There is more reality than poetry in a life on the Tented field.'

Nor did they correctly anticipate the scale and scope of combat. Entering battle with severe misperceptions, the killing, the maiming, and the destruction caught men on both sides unprepared. Many had visions of personal and group glory, which realities abruptly banished from their minds. 'I can inform you that I have Seen the Monkey Show at last,' a Confederate penned home after Stones River, 'and I dont Waunt to see it no more.' He went on to describe, 'Som had there hedes shot of[f] and som ther armes and legs Won was Shot in too in the midel.' He then concluded with exasperation, 'I can tell you that I am tirde of Ware.'

They were nothing more than livestock in a butcher's pen, herded forward for the slaughter by what seemed like uncaring and incompetent generals. Men in the prime of their lives were cut down indiscriminately. Friends and comrades fell on their left and right, leaving those who survived to puzzle over the question: why them? And while they may have won the battle, rarely did they advance the cause dramatically. There seemed to be no end in sight.

Eventually, that experience in camp, on the march, and in battle hardened men on both sides. They learned how to conduct themselves better on the battlefield and in camp, to husband valuable resources and to discipline themselves on important matters. Soldiers accrued some emotional immunity to the randomness of the killing and the brutality of warfare, realizing that fear and intensive examination would produce no results. They resigned themselves to the idea that it was either God's will or their time.

The men of 1861 and 1862 had become veterans, with a vast warehouse of military knowledge based on personal experience or observation. 'The experience of twenty years peaceful life,' noted a veteran on the anniversary of his first battle, 'has been crowded into three years.' After just a few years, so stated another enlisted man, he and his comrades 'had learned nearly all that was worth knowing, at least far more than [our] generals knew three years before.'

Since early childhood, family and society had taught them to make decisions for themselves, to act as they saw best. Veterans did not hesitate to put those hard-earned military lessons to good use, even without supervision of their officers. They mastered the art of selecting excellent tactical positions and throwing up breastworks to shield their bodies from the accurate fire of rifled muskets. Engineers marveled at the positions and fortifications that enlisted men built quickly and on their own initiative. While killing was an inextricable component of warfare, soldiers learned how to take steps to reduce risks, to preserve themselves and their comrades for another day. Early in the war, they advanced elbow to elbow, as the tactics manual had instructed them. As veterans, they realized that the purpose was to concentrate firepower and strength, but they could accomplish that by dispersing themselves a little more and exploiting terrain features and cover. Yet they retained the important objective: to focus their fire on specific targets and areas. In camp and on the march, they knew 'just what to do and what not to do.' They practiced good hygiene, and supplemented their diet from the countryside. As one sergeant in Sherman's army commented, 'I believe if we were as green as we were when we first came out – (as the 'Vets' say) we would starve to death.' Almost as important, veterans could teach these lessons to new troops. While they liked to play pranks and mislead newcomers, the hardened soldiers also understood that their own lives depended to some degree on how well the green soldiers performed, and they would not neglect the instruction of any who would listen.

Along with changes in behavior, veterans embraced new attitudes about the war. They began to see both soldiers and civilians as the enemy, and they recognized the destruction of property as a powerful tool in fighting the war. Rebel cavalry commander Nathan Bedford Forrest proved himself master of the destructive cavalry raid, wreaking such havoc on garrisons, railroads, and supply depots that Sherman called him 'that devil Forrest.' Confederates, too, paid less credence to notions of 'civilized warfare,' especially when it came to black soldiers. Both they and the black troops fought under the black flag, signaling their opponent that they would give no quarter, nor expect any. All too often, they executed those they captured.

While Confederates in the Western Theater exhibited that change in attitude about the war, they did not have nearly as many opportunities as the Federals to implement it. Union soldiers campaigned throughout the South and, eventually, they came to the conclusion that by making Southern whites suffer, they could contribute mightily to the war effort. In part, Northerners felt a sense of hostility over secessionists' efforts to destroy a wonderful union, but as veterans they also came around to see the linkage between the home front and the men in the field. Confederates certainly exhibited tremendous loyalty to their cause, fighting for years under adverse conditions on meager rations and in skimpy clothing. Yet the Yankees realized that many Rebel opponents had a greater loyalty than that cause – the one to their families. If Federal troops could make life miserable for loved ones at home, they would force Confederate soldiers to choose between their responsibility to their families and their obligations to their government. As Union armies penetrated deeper into the Confederacy, consuming food, confiscating slaves and other property, and terrifying the Southern people, more and more Rebels left the ranks to care for their loved ones.

By the last year and a half of the war, these Union and Confederate troops had mastered the art and science of soldiering. Those who remained in ranks had toughened their bodies by fighting off diseases. They had learned to deal with harsh elements, to march great distances and to live amid plenty or on little subsistence. In short, these citizens had learned to think, to act, to feel, and to fight like veteran soldiers.

Black soldiers

Early in the war, abolitionists and African-Americans urged the Lincoln administration to accept blacks for uniformed service. The President declined. He had more white volunteers than he was authorized by Congress to accept, and the Union was walking a tightrope with the Border States. Black enlistment might have driven them to the Confederacy.

Blacks, however, began to take matters into their own hands. By the end of April 1861, several slaves whom Rebels had employed in constructing defense works slipped away and sought sanctuary at Fort Monroe, Virginia. When a Confederate officer came to retrieve the runaways, Brigadier-General Benjamin Butler, a prewar lawyer and politician, refused. Federal law did not apply to Rebels, Butler explained. Furthermore, slaves had aided the Confederate army and were subject to confiscation as contraband of war. Butler then employed the runaways to build a bakery for Federal troops. In one decisive moment, Butler had freed slaves and hired them to work for the Union army. Four

The overwhelming majority of black soldiers, perhaps 150,000 of the nearly 180,000, came from slavery. Often they fled from the fields as Union armies passed nearby, or they undertook a risky trek to locate Federal lines. Here two photographs expose the uplifting nature of military service. In one, we see a boy in his slave clothes; in the other, he has transformed into a drummer boy for the US army. (Left, Library of Congress; Right, US Army)

months later, Congress endorsed Butler's policy in the First Confiscation Act.

As the Union forces penetrated into the Confederacy, more and more slaves entered their camps. Many Federal officers objected to the idea of returning slaves, especially to owners in seceded states, and the practice distracted military personnel from their primary duty of suppressing the rebellion. In early 1862, the War Department prohibited the use of soldiers in retrieving slaves. The institution of slavery broke down a bit more.

After the failure of McClellan's campaign against Richmond in mid-1862, Lincoln re-evaluated his approach to the war. Recruiting had slowed to a trickle, and the largest untapped resource, African-Americans, was not being exploited. Slavery, moreover, had been the basis of secession, and the enemy had used slaves to help their cause. If the Union planned to prosecute the war fully, it must take slaves away from the Rebels and employ them for the Federal Government, both in and out of uniform. And if Northerners hoped eventually to bring the seceded states back into the Union, they must put that one unsolvable problem, slavery, on the road to extinction. Lincoln determined to issue an Emancipation Proclamation and to recruit blacks as soldiers.

For these controversial decisions, the President had tacit support from Congress.

Aware that Federal forces were their ticket to freedom, slaves began fleeing to Union troops whenever they approached nearby. Often they grabbed whatever they could carry, but in this case the refugees were able to use a wagon and horses to convey them to freedom. (Library of Congress)

On 17 July 1862, Congress passed the Second Confiscation Act, which authorized the President to confiscate all slaves of Rebels. That same day, Congress adopted the Militia Act, which permitted Lincoln to employ blacks for any military duties that he believed they were competent to perform. Lincoln also justified emancipation by his powers as commander in chief. Slaves aided the Rebel war effort. Surely he could deprive them of their use. As it turned out, Lincoln decided to await the next major Union victory, which did not occur until September 1862 at Antietam, before issuing the proclamation. But that summer, he began bringing African-Americans into uniform.

The first black soldiers came from a New Orleans militia unit, the 1st Louisiana Native Guards. The Native Guards had black company-grade officers and even a black major. Several months later, the Union recruited the first black regiment from scratch, the 1st South Carolina (Colored) Infantry, later called the 33rd US Colored Infantry, with all white officers.

The idea of putting blacks in uniform was extremely controversial. To increase the policy's acceptability, the administration sought competent whites to command these soldiers. By the end of the war, well over 7,000 whites had received commissions in the United States Colored Troops, while only 125 or so blacks were made officers.

Although black abolitionist Frederick Douglass and others promised that blacks would make excellent soldiers, it was essential for these first regiments to fight well. And they did. At Port Hudson, the 1st and 3rd Louisiana Native Guards charged Confederate works valiantly, and suffered heavy losses. After a New York Times newspaperman witnessed the attack, the paper declared, 'It is no longer possible to doubt the bravery and steadiness of the colored race, when rightly led.'

Several weeks later, black soldiers participated in a brutal fight at Milliken's Bend, Louisiana. The black regiments had only a few days of training and many had never fired their rifles. In a vicious assault by

368   FRANK LESLIE'S ILLUSTRATED NEWSPAPER.   [Oct. 26, 1861.

The issue of whether to employ blacks as soldiers was hotly contested. Despite the assertion of Frederick Douglass and other African-Americans that they would make efficient troops, the Northern white public was skeptical. Here, a powerfully racist cartoon in a popular magazine expresses the belief that blacks could contribute little to the army. (*Frank Leslie's Illustrated Newspaper*)

overwhelming Confederate numbers, the white soldiers fled but the black troops stood fast. Even though they could not reload and fire effectively, they fought hand to hand and ultimately repulsed the Rebels. One black regiment suffered the highest percentage of men killed in a single battle for the entire war. 'I never more wish to hear the expression, "The niggers wont fight,"' proclaimed a white officer in the fight.

The final event that secured a place for black soldiers was the intrepid assault by the 54th Massachusetts (Colored) Infantry on Fort Wagner, South Carolina. The 54th was the brainchild of the governor of Massachusetts, and it was raised in the North with tremendous publicity. Abolitionists or their sons served as officers. Among the enlisted ranks were two of Douglass's sons.

Its colonel, Robert Gould Shaw, volunteered the regiment to spearhead the attack on the fort that helped to guard Charleston harbor. Against a withering fire, the 54th carried up to and into the fort, yet, ultimately, the defenders repulsed them. Among the 40 percent casualties that the 54th suffered was its commander, Shaw, whom Rebels gleefully announced was 'buried with his niggers.' For the second time, newspapermen witnessed the attack, and the battle received extensive coverage in the North.

Having proved their worth on the battlefield, black soldiers began to convert detractors in and out of the army into supporters. By the end of the war, almost 179,000 blacks had served in the Union army and another 20,000 had enlisted in the navy. Military service was a thrilling event in their lives, especially for former slaves. 'I felt like a man,' recalled one black soldier, 'with a uniform on and a gun in my hand.' It gave blacks, free and slave, a sense of belonging to the United States.

Black soldiers and sailors fought to destroy slavery and restore the Union, and they hoped that a grateful nation would

reward them for their devotion by giving them full and equal rights in the postwar world. Their sense of commitment sustained them through extensive discrimination by the Union army and acts of brutality, such as the Fort Pillow massacre in Tennessee, by Confederates.

At peak, one in every eight Union soldiers was black; the percentage of black sailors was even higher. Black troops fought on 41 major battlefields and in 449 minor engagements. Sixteen soldiers and seven sailors received Medals of Honor for valor. Some 37,000 blacks in an army uniform gave their lives, and untold sailors did, too. Lincoln paid them high compliments when he declared that black soldiers fought as well as whites, and that their service was indispensable to victory.

Eventually black soldiers received an opportunity to prove themselves in combat. It was only on the field of battle that they could demonstrate their manhood and earn the postwar rights that they coveted. (Library of Congress)

'Keep it and you can save the Union,' he wrote. 'Throw it away, and the Union goes with it.'

Perhaps the greatest tribute to black soldiers, though, was paid by their opponents. Desperate for manpower, the Confederacy narrowly elected to enlist its own black soldiers in the waning months of the war. Critical in the adoption of the policy was a statement from General Robert E. Lee, in which he argued that the Union had employed black troops with success and he believed they would make 'efficient soldiers.'

Prisoners of war

In a strange way, both Grant's Vicksburg campaign and the recruitment of black soldiers negatively influenced conditions in Civil War prison camps. Neither the Union nor the Confederacy had prepared well for the massive influx of prisoners that occurred in the last two years of the war. In the first year, only a small number of soldiers were captured. Numbers escalated in the second year of fighting, and both governments threw up prison camps until they could exchange them. In 1863, however, this exchange broke down. Confederates refused to treat black soldiers and their white officers as prisoners of war, insisting that former slaves return into bondage and their officers be prosecuted for inciting servile insurrection. The unwillingness of Confederates to include black troops in any exchange program dissolved the cartel. Confederates, moreover, declared the paroles issued by Grant to Rebel soldiers at Vicksburg invalid and placed quite a number of these parolees back in the ranks without

exchanging them properly. In protest, the Federal Government refused to swap prisoners, and for much of the next two years, the number of prisoners on both sides mounted.

Since no one anticipated the breakdown of the cartel, the huge influx of captives from the 1863 and 1864 campaigns caught them unprepared. The Confederates, for example, erected Andersonville because they feared the Union army might overrun the camp on the James River in Virginia. They chose the Andersonville location for its isolation. Originally laid out on 16 acres (6.5ha) for 10,000 prisoners, they eventually expanded it to 26 acres (10.5ha). Ultimately, Andersonville served as the home for 45,000 Union soldiers, with a peak number at

As Sherman's troops passed through Millen, Georgia, the soldiers discovered an abandoned prisoner-of-war camp called Camp Lawton. Prisoners had to burrow into the ground for shelter, and they had to remain inside a 'dead line,' which was still visible. If prisoners crossed over the line, they were shot. The sight outraged Sherman's army, which also discovered a similar prison camp outside Columbia, South Carolina. (Author's collection)

The most notorious of the Civil War prison camps was the stockade at Andersonville, Georgia. Originally planned for 10,000, it was home to more than three times that number, resulting in severe overcrowding, sanitary problems, and disease. (Collection of the New York Historical Society)

33,000. Amid the filth, congestion, lack of shelter, and poor water supply, some 13,000 died there.

Large Federal prison camps existed at Point Lookout, Maryland; Elmira, New York; Camp Chase, Ohio; and Johnson's Island, Illinois. Although Elmira earned the worst reputation among Confederate prisoners, the conditions there were better than at Andersonville. Elmira housed less than one-third the number of inmates on over 60 percent more acreage. The Union also erected barracks to shelter the inmates from the brutal cold of a Central New York winter. Still, Elmira had a staggering

24 percent death rate for Rebel soldiers incarcerated there.

No doubt, more intelligent planning and effort on both sides would have alleviated much of the misery in these camps. Of the 195,000 Union prisoners of war, more than 30,000 died. Federals held 215,000 Confederates, 26,000 of whom perished. Nor did these figures include all those who endured severe or chronic ailments from prolonged hardships and exposure. Yet despite postwar accusations, neither the Union nor the Confederacy deliberately intended to inflict horrible suffering on their captives. Rebel prison camps tended to be worse than Federal pens, but Confederate soldiers fared worse than Yankees. If the Confederacy struggled to feed and clothe its own fighting men, it should have surprised no one that its prisoners would fare poorly.

William Wilbur Edgerton

'What storyes I shall have to tell when I get home,' announced Private William Wilbur Edgerton to his mother. Born and reared in Central New York, the third of four children to Dorothy Doud and John Leffingwell Edgerton, Wilbur had enlisted in the 107th New York Volunteer Infantry illegally in July 1862, just one month shy of his seventeenth birthday.

From a tender young age, Wilbur had been on his own. His father was a ne'er do well who wandered about, searching for success and happiness, never to find it. Wilbur's two older sisters married, and his mother, financially abandoned, took the youngest boy to Sparta, Wisconsin, where she had friends. Wilbur bonded well with his mother, recalling, 'When I was a little boy, I tought nothing was so nice as to sit on mothers lap and I have not exatly [gotten] over that.'

The best thing that ever happened to him, he believed, was being thrown out to his own devices at such an early age. Wilbur started kicking around at various jobs at twelve – fiddle playing, a cooper, a farm hand, a factory worker, and then a blacksmith. Neither fiddling nor work as a cooper paid much, so he took on employment with a farmer. When the man ripped him off of nearly half his pay, he stormed off and entered factory labor. Wilbur left that to apprentice with a blacksmith, which at the time offered a much better career track. 'Blacksmithing is black work,' he conveyed to his mother in racially charged language common in that day, 'but it brings white money so I dont care.' Unfortunately, the blacksmith's explosive temper and vulgar ways convinced him to quit. He then linked up with another blacksmith; this time a good, decent man.

Edgerton enlisted for the simple reason that everyone kept asking him why he did not soldier. He was a young man, without family, in good health, and because he had been on his own so long, everyone assumed he was older than he really was. 'I made up my mind that it was my duty to fight for my country and I did so,' Edgerton justified.

Just two and a half months after the regiment was formed, the 107th New York 'saw the elephant' in the single bloodiest day of the war, at Antietam in Maryland. Lee had raided into Maryland, but his plans fell into Federal hands. When Union forces moved more aggressively against him than he anticipated, Lee retreated to the north bank of the Potomac River, near a town called Sharpsburg and a creek named Antietam. On the morning of 17 September 1862, the 107th advanced through the North Woods and into the timber, where they came under fire for the first time. As they rushed into the East Woods, a Rebel volley struck down men on either side of Edgerton. You 'have no idea what it is to be a souldier off in a strang country whare your comrades are a dieing off fast and no noing how soon before your time will come,' he explained to his younger brother. In the course of passing through the woods, 'I run over a good maney ded and wounded *Rebels*.'

A couple of hours later, the 107th advanced to protect an artillery battery. 'The balls flew around my head like hail stones and sounded like a swarm of bees,' he described to his brother. 'O Johney I tell you that you can have no conception of the thouths [thoughts] that run through a mans head about thouse times it made a man think of the good and the bad things that he ever did in his life. I know my head was full of thoughts.' People who had been in combat had tried to prepare him for it, but the experience was nothing like anything he had ever witnessed. 'I have heard it said that after the first volley that you forged [forget] all the dainger,' he elaborated. 'Unless a man is scart out of his rite sences he knowes what is going on as well as he did at first.' Still, combat affected him. 'I know that my flesh tickeld and flinched all the time expecting to feel a ball pierce it.'

Two days later, his regiment had to cross over the hotly contested battlefield in pursuit of the Rebels. 'Sutch a odor (politely speaking) I never heard tell of *nor ever do I want smell it again,*' he confessed. 'The dead layed in heaps well it made me so sick that I had to fall out and laydown beside the road.' Despite this vivid depiction, the young private felt he had failed to convey a true sense of the experience. 'It is no usee,' he insisted, 'woords have not enuf meening.'

In mid-1863, the 107th New York fought in two of the greatest battles of the war, Chancellorsville and Gettysburg, and Edgerton was right in the thick of them. At Chancellorsville, Confederate General Stonewall Jackson launched a brilliant flank attack that rolled up the Union XI Corps and threatened the rear of the XII, to which the 107th was assigned. In the course of the fighting, Edgerton had his percussion cap box shot off, and a Rebel ball passed through his cap. 'I wouldent sware that I kiled aney body,' he admitted to his father, 'but I am pretty shore that a good maney were hit buy me fore the most of the time they were not more than 10 or 15 rods [55–82.5yds; 50–75m] off and I know that I can hit a hat 20 rods off every time for I have tride it so you can judg for your self.'

At Gettysburg two months later, the battle 'was as hard if not harder than aney other that I have been in.' At one point, a shell fragment knocked his rifle right out of his hand. Having fought in several major battles, Edgerton had begun to develop some seasoning in combat. 'I mad[e] up my mind that if *they* wanted me to stop fighting *hit me* fir they couldent *scare* me aney,' he told his mother after Gettysburg.

Just before Antietam, his best friend, John Wiggins, deserted, only to return under Lincoln's amnesty the next April. Edgerton helped his friend, who had a family at home, by lending him money, but he would never have entertained that kind of conduct himself. 'I dont care about fighting,' he confessed after Chancellorsville. 'I would willingly give all I am *worth* and a *good deal more if I had it to be out of this scrape,* but never the less I am no *coward* and I *never* will *disgrace* the *name* of *Edgerton* by *desertion* or *Sneeking* out of *danger* like some have.'

That fall of 1863, after the Union disaster at Chickamauga, the War Department transferred the XI and XII Corps under Major-General Joseph Hooker to Chattanooga. It was an extraordinary logistical achievement; Edgerton and his comrades endured the 'rufiest rideing' and a derailment, but they made it in time to witness the rout of Bragg's army. For a change, the 107th saw little action, but the regiment's arrival marked a dramatic change for its men. Not until the war's end would they return to Virginia. They soon became part of the Western Army, with the XI and XII merged to form the XX Corps under Hooker.

Because of his service in both theaters, Edgerton offered some valuable insights into the way that the enemy fought. Federal commanders, he noticed, preserved the lives of their men better by placing greater emphasis on artillery fire. The Rebels, with inferior artillery, compensated with aggressive infantry. 'There is one thing that our goverment does that suits me to a dot,' he instructed his mother, 'that is we fight mostly with Artillery, The Rebls fight mostly with Infantry. They fight as though a mans life was not worth one sent or in other words with desperation.' He also believed that the western Rebels did not fight as well as Lee's troops. Around Chattanooga, he knew that the Federals confronted what he described as two-fifths of Lee's army, including two of Longstreet's divisions, 'the best fighting men the World ever saw.' Weeks after the Union crushed Bragg's army without Longstreet's troops present, Edgerton measured the performance of Confederate eastern and western troops and concluded, 'The rebels in this country are not such fighting men as they are in Va. [Virginia].'

The hardships of campaigning and general military service wore him out, yet he refused to let them drag his morale down too far. 'Oh if I ever do get home I know I will enjoy myself,' he vowed to his mother. 'You will never hear me grumble.' Food was always substandard. He estimated to his sister that rain-soaked clothes, blankets, and knapsacks weighed about 100lb (45kg), and that a soldier on the march hauled a woolen blanket, a rubber blanket, a change of underclothes, a tent, a knapsack, three days' rations, a belt, and a rifle. In addition to combat, everyday duty exacted quite a toll from the men. As Edgerton walked guard duty in rain, high winds, and hail, 'I would satisfy my self buy saing, that it was all for the *union*.'

As he traveled more and more throughout the South, the New Yorker gained greater exposure to the institution of slavery. 'It looks horrible,' he wrote his mother. He detested the idea of people held in bondage, some of whom were as white as he was. Slavery, he felt, made Southern whites somewhat lazy. 'I am and always was an Abolitionist,' he claimed, 'and I guess I am on the right side.'

That spring, 1864, the Union army under the overall leadership of Grant determined to press the Confederates on every front, with the two major operations targeting Richmond and Atlanta. As campaign season approached, Edgerton did not want to go forward, but duty compelled him to do so. 'Of course we dont like to fight but then, if nesesary, why, there is no body knows how aney better than we do,' he elaborated to his mother. 'I shant expose myself unnesisaryly, neither shall I shirk from doing my duty as a soldier.' Just before the campaign opened, he and Wiggins had their photograph taken together. 'I dont feel very patriotic this morning for we have got to march to morrow to the frunt & I dont want to go,' he admitted to his brother. But go he did.

Sherman had to maintain continual contact with the Rebel army under Johnston, to prevent wide flank attacks or the movement of reinforcements elsewhere, while at the same time enabling the Federals to turn the Confederates from their defensive positions. As a result, Edgerton and his comrades remained under fire nearly the entire campaign, occupying positions anywhere from 200 to 500yds (180–450m) away. In the fight at Dallas on 28 May 1864, Edgerton declared it 'the hottest plase I was ever in' – strong words from someone who had fought in the thick of battle at Antietam, Chancellorsville, and Gettysburg. His regiment lost 168 men that day. Throughout June, he reported numerous close calls. 'I have again been preserved from the leden missles of death, while so maney of my comrades have fallen,' he alerted his mother in late June. After assessing the hardships of the campaign, he announced, 'It is a wounder [wonder] to me that I am alive.'

On 14 June, a cocky Wilbur Edgerton notified his mother, 'The rebls here dont know how to fight & they never will.' Less than two months later, a Confederate sharpshooter drilled him in the right shoulder with a minie ball outside Atlanta. Edgerton went to the field hospital, where he recovered in short order and returned to his command, just in time to participate in the fall of Atlanta. When Sherman swung his army to the southwest of the city, to sever the last open rail connections, he left the XX Corps to guard his own railroad supply line. As Hood vacated the city, the Federals pushed into Atlanta, with the 107th among the first to enter. 'Atlanta is ours,' Edgerton crowed to his mother, knowing full well the consequences of that victory.

Throughout the Atlanta campaign, the upcoming presidential election seldom strayed far from the minds of Edgerton and his comrades. Nearly all of them supported Lincoln's re-election bid, even if they were too young to vote, as was Edgerton. 'Our army is full of animation, patriotism &c. [etc.],' he assessed to his mother in early July. '[We] Have a determination to settle this war before next Presidential election for fear of copperhead being elected.' He predicted, 'if Lincoln is reelected next fall the War will end.' Several weeks later, he announced, 'I am for the administration as it is & for an unconditional surrender or extermination of the rebles.' The fall of Atlanta virtually assured that re-election. Still, he pledged his commitment to the Union and all for which it stood. 'I would die far sooner than have it destroyed,' he wrote.

By mid-November 1864, Edgerton and the other 65,000 men in Sherman's two armies had begun their lengthy trek to Savannah. The 107th passed through Milledgeville, the capital of Georgia, where some men held mock proceedings and left the capitol building a mess. Foraging parties gathered food and fodder from the countryside, while soldiers wrecked railroads and anything else of military value. By Christmas time, they had seized Savannah.

Throughout the Georgia campaign and the occupation duty in Savannah, Edgerton expanded his contacts with Southern women. Generally, he had few problems. Their penchant for chewing tobacco disgusted him, and he felt they lacked the intellectual snap of Northern women, but if Union soldiers behaved properly, they responded with respect. In Savannah, they sold meals and other items to soldiers, and the interactions were quite informative. Most Southern white women supported the rebellion, Edgerton thought, because they believed the Federal army would take away their slaves, which of course was true. 'Now that they are going to lose their niggers they dont know what to do,' he explained.

In late January 1865, after a much-needed rest, the army set out once again, this time northward for North Carolina, a campaign that proved much more demanding than the march to Savannah. In addition to stronger Confederate opposition, the topography, winter rains, and scarcity of food took a greater toll on Edgerton and his comrades. After a few days in South Carolina, he announced, 'This

country is nothing but swamps, swamps, swamps.' Along the way, he saw old, worn-out plantations overgrown by woods and underbrush. Although his regiment marched around Columbia, he passed through Fayetteville, North Carolina, which housed a major Confederate arsenal. There, he assessed the campaign as 'the hardest of the war.' Throughout South Carolina, the troops had to forage for their food in a land of scattered farms and plantations. 'Some have went hungry for a long time,' he commented to his mother, 'but *Will* has had plenty to eat.' At Averasborough, North Carolina, the 107th exchanged shots with the Rebels, suffering 27 men wounded.

This is the scene of the Battle of New Hope Church, or Dallas, in late May 1864 during the Atlanta campaign. Private Wilbur Edgerton, a veteran of Antietam, Chancellorsville, and Gettysburg, declared it 'the hottest plase I was ever in.' (Library of Congress)

The only other men the regiment lost in the Carolinas campaign were 19 foragers whom Confederate cavalry and guerrillas captured.

Several days after the army reached Goldsboro, North Carolina, Edgerton announced to his mother, 'I am so sick of soldering that my patriotism is below par.' Fortunately, the war did not last much longer. In April, Sherman's army advanced, and just as quickly it halted for negotiations. By the end of the month, the Confederates had surrendered, and the 107th New York began its march for Washington, DC. On 24 May, it proudly participated in the Grand Review along Pennsylvania Avenue, with the President, Grant, Sherman, and others in attendance. Three and a half weeks later, Wilbur Edgerton had purchased a new suit of civilian clothes and began work in a store. He received an honorable discharge on 18 June 1865.

In the years after the war, Edgerton tried his hand at a variety of occupations. He graduated from medical school and practiced in Kansas and Missouri. Eventually, he gave that up for jobs as a merchant and a banker in Wheeling, Missouri. The father of three children, he became a prominent member of the community, even serving as mayor of the town. Fittingly, he died on Armistice Day (now called Veteran's Day), 11 November 1931.

The home fronts

The Northern home front

Opposition to the war gained a big boost from the Emancipation Proclamation and the employment of black soldiers. Peace Democrats, nicknamed 'Copperheads,' hated the notion of fighting a war against Southern whites over slavery. Better to let them leave the Union, they argued, than spill white men's blood over the status of black people. Not only did Copperheads rail against the Lincoln administration and its war policy, some also encouraged individuals to desert the armed forces or resist enforcement of wartime measures. Many Union supporters blamed the Copperheads for the 200,000 men who deserted the Federal blue during the war.

Along with emancipation, the administration policy that generated the harshest criticism was conscription. First begun in 1862 as a kind of quota system, it became necessary to strengthen the recruitment process when enlistment fell off in 1862 and 1863. Although the procedure changed slightly during the war, essentially all males from 20 to 45 had to enroll. If a congressional district failed to reach its manpower quota when the government called for new troops, lots would be drawn to determine who would report. Once the individual selected passed a physical, he could serve, purchase a commutation for $300, or hire a substitute. Rather than suffer through a draft, communities raised money as enlistment bounties to entice volunteers, who would count against the quota. Others joined in insurance programs that purchased a commutation.

Conscription generated only 46,000 draftees who entered the army, and it caused considerable disaffection among Northerners. The commutation and substitute process led to charges of a rich man's war and a poor man's fight, and in several cities draft resistance evolved into riots. Yet the administration saw conscription as a carrot and stick approach, hoping to spur enlistment. From that perspective, it succeeded, since the Lincoln administration assembled enough troops to win the war.

Throughout the war, close to two and a quarter million served in Federal blue, and at peak, the Union had over one million men in uniform at one time. These military personnel had to be clothed, fed, equipped, and paid. As civilians, they were both producers and consumers; as soldiers and sailors, they grew or manufactured nothing, yet consumed massively.

Somehow, the North had to compensate for the manpower losses to the armed forces. Immigrants arrived, but in general the movement of people from Europe slowed down during the war. To fill the void, the Union relied heavily on two sources: women and mechanization. Females took to the fields, factories, and shops to produce the enormous amounts of food and other products to meet the needs of the domestic and the military market. The North also depended on labor-saving equipment to offset the loss of workers. Despite rising prices and income, a huge increase in the production of farm machinery kept the price low, making reapers and other farm implements more affordable. In various industries, too, owners adopted machinery to replace skilled or semi-skilled laborers whom they could no longer find. By the end of the war, the North had actually increased the amount of foodstuffs it grew – so much so that it fed its armies and the folks at home and exported large amounts to Europe – and was producing a sufficient amount of clothing, consumer goods, and war material to meet domestic needs and fuel the war machine.

Still, the absence of husbands and sons placed an enormous strain on families. Without the labor of a valued son or the family's father, parents and especially women had to fill unusual roles and take on added work. Often, neighbors helped each other, and communal organizations tried to soften the burden. Yet primarily, family members had to rely on each other. They picked up the slack and rallied in support of their loved ones in military service, working their way through tough times and encouraging those in uniform to do their duty.

While soldiers and sailors battled their Confederate counterparts, people on the home front warred as best they could against rising prices. The Lincoln government taxed its citizens heavily, but it financed much of the war through the sale of war bonds and the printing of paper notes. The flood of money and limitation on supplies of labor, raw materials, and finished goods drove prices up to double their prewar level, and in some instances even higher. Farmers, at least, produced their own food; inflation placed a huge burden on workers with fixed wages.

Despite the magnitude of the war, it did not suck all traditional impulses from society. Children still attended school, colleges remained open, individuals sought comfort in places of worship, and people fulfilled all sorts of needs in their communities. But the war also promoted a kind of voluntarism that did focus on the war and its consequences. Women sewed clothing for loved ones and strangers, people at home wrote millions of letters to maintain the bond between war front and home front, and tens of thousands flocked to sanitary fairs to raise money for the care and physical and spiritual well-being of the troops. In short, victory required a military and a civilian effort.

The Southern home front

Most of the men in Rebel service in 1861 had enlisted for a solitary year, and as the term neared a close, the Confederacy confronted the prospect of its army melting away. In desperation, it passed the first Conscription Act in American history in April 1862. The law applied to men from 18 to 35 and allowed for occupational exemptions and the hiring of substitutes. The object was to spur enlistment with the conscription whip. By September 1862, the Rebel Congress had raised the upper limit to 45 years of age. It also yielded to pressure from wealthy slave owners to keep home white males who could control the slave population. The Twenty-Negro Law permitted one exemption per 20 slaves whom the master owned, and it fueled the contention in the seceded states of a rich man's war and a poor man's fight, as in the North. Like the Federal law, conscription stirred opposition, but it also helped to fill the ranks. From a total white population of approximately 5.5 million, perhaps 900,000 men served in the Confederate army, and at peak the Confederacy had about 450,000 men in uniform.

With such an extraordinary percentage of white males in service, comparatively few able-bodied white men remained at home to run farms, fabricate goods, and supervise the slaves, whose productive labors were more important than ever. In many instances, women had to rise to the occasion and take over for loved ones. Yet discipline and force were the principal means of controlling the 3.5 million slave laborers, and without many adult white males around, bondsmen regularly tested the resolve of women and elderly or youthful male owners and overseers.

It did not take slaves long to learn about the war and emancipation. They realized that any work slowdown or disruption on the plantation impaired productivity, thereby hurting the Rebel cause and enhancing the possibility of freedom becoming a reality. Slave-owning wives wrote to soldiers, complaining of slave insolence, resistant attitudes, or flight to Union lines. From hundreds of miles away, soldiers could only advise. Nevertheless, that frustration, and the ever-present fear of servile insurrection, lingered in their minds throughout the war, and worries distracted them from the business at hand, war making.

Since a majority of Southerners were farmers or planters before the war, their absence cut deeply into agricultural productivity. The Confederacy had to feed the same number of mouths, but with fewer workers, and as the Union army advanced, the Confederacy had to do so on less and less tillable acreage. The Confederate government encouraged individuals to grow more food crops and less cotton, but shortages in the army and in numerous areas of the Confederacy still occurred, leading to protests and even riots.

Refugees from the war flooded cities, seeking protection, jobs, and nourishment. The population of Richmond soared almost out of control; in other cities, it increased astronomically as well. Columbia, South Carolina, for instance, tripled in size over the four years. The local infrastructure lacked the capacity to care for the huge influx, and prices began to skyrocket. Nor did the paper currency, which the Davis administration printed to finance much of the war, help inflation. By the late stages of the war, these paper notes were more valuable as keepsakes than as a medium of exchange.

While prices rose substantially everywhere in the Confederacy, urban areas suffered the greatest escalation. In 1864, corn sold at $20 a bushel in Charleston. By early the next year, it cost $40 per bushel in nearby Columbia, and $25 per bushel in Athens, Georgia. Bacon, a Southern staple, normally sold for 12 cents per pound (0.45kg). By 1865, the prices ranged from $2 to $4 per pound, and were even higher in some areas. Emma LeConte, a 17-year-old South Carolinian, reported that homespun cloth cost $8–10 per yard (0.91m) and calico between $20 and $30. Her parents bought her shoes for $150. A load of firewood, she recorded, went for $100. How poor people survived is a virtual mystery.

Because prices escalated on an almost daily basis, and currency lacked any real value, farmers declined to sell to the government, which would only pay anywhere from one-third to one-eighth of the market price. In order to feed the troops, commissaries confiscated food and livestock, which again alienated farmers. Even then, the Commissary Department procured so little food, and the transportation network had fallen into such decline, that the Confederacy provided less than a third of the standard authorized ration for its troops.

The consequences of war on the Confederacy's home soil, too, took their toll. As Union armies penetrated deeper into the seceded states, they disrupted more and more lives. Soldiers on either side took food wherever they found it, leaving civilians in dire straits. And when Sherman, Sheridan, and others launched raiding marches, seizing food from the countryside and destroying anything of military value, they left those civilians in their wake in horrible circumstances.

Ultimately, this raiding strategy forced Confederates onto a spiral of defeat. Civilians wrote to soldiers, explaining their plight and compelling these men in uniform to choose between their family and their country. Many deserted to care for loved ones. On the way back, they had to take food from farms, which burdened other civilians, and their collective absence dramatically weakened the Rebel armies in the field. With insufficient manpower, Confederates could not check Yankee advances, which in turn exposed more Rebel families to the ravages of Union troops. That prompted more Confederates to leave the ranks to care for family members in need.

Once the spiral began, the Confederates could not halt it. The experiences of the Confederate States of America powerfully illustrate the intricate link between armies in the field and civilians on the home front.

Emma LeConte

'Reunion! Good Heavens!' exclaimed 17-year-old Emma LeConte about the prospects of peace with those vandals, the Yankees. 'How we hate with the whole strength and depth of our souls.'

Born in Georgia and raised in Columbia, South Carolina, Emma was the daughter of a science professor at the College of South Carolina, later renamed the University of South Carolina. From this privileged background, she received a world-class education for a young woman in her day. Her upbringing bound her intricately to the cultural trappings of Southern society, and her youthful and unyielding passion for the Confederacy reflected broad sentiments among the well-to-do people in South Carolina.

Just a handful of blocks away from her home on campus grounds, South Carolinians celebrated secession from the Union. Emma recalled with delight the moment she and her neighbors learned that Fort Sumter had capitulated. They were seated in her father's library when the bell at the marketplace clanged, announcing a momentous event. Everyone rushed outside, where they heard the news. 'The whole town was in joyful tumult,' she described. Men ushered off to war. Women filled the void in all sorts of ways and contributed to the war effort by supporting the cause, caring for the ill and injured, and enduring any sacrifice necessary for victory.

Emma never doubted the justice of the Confederate cause. Despite her exceptional education in mathematics, science, French, German, philosophy, literature, and history, she did not challenge the notions that blacks were inferior beings and that slavery benefited the African race. The Northern states threatened to undermine the institution of slavery and impose themselves and their ideas on the Southern people. No self-respecting individual, no free person, could justly endure such a humiliation. The North attempted to enslave them, and Southern whites dissolved their connection to the Union. God and justice – inseparably intertwined in her mind and those of fellow secessionists – were on their side.

But by the end of 1864, the prospects looked bleak. Lee and his valiant army had locked in a life-and-death struggle outside Petersburg and Richmond. Sherman's army had swept through Georgia, leaving desolation in its wake. Savannah had capitulated. And 'Sherman the brute avows his intention of converting South Carolina into a wilderness,' she feared.

Even before the Federal army turned northward, it threatened Emma's family. Her 15-year-old sister Sallie, her aunt, and two cousins resided on a plantation 25 miles (40km) south of Savannah. In December, Emma's father, who worked during much of the war for the Nitre and Mining Bureau, embarked on a lengthy trek to find and bring them back to Columbia. While she waited, reports reached her ears on the conditions in Georgia. How would they survive without provisions, she wondered. In her diary, she worried over 'how dreadfully they must have been frightened.' With her father traveling into harm's way, the thought of his death instilled a sense of terror in her. By 7 February 1865, he had brought them all back to Columbia, but in doing so, he had unwittingly moved from an area beyond Sherman's swath to a primary target.

The war had taken its toll on the LeConte family's quality of life, too. Although they were well off financially, skyrocketing inflation, a relatively tight Union blockade, and limited supplies forced them to cut back drastically. The family ate two meals a day.

They had two plates of bread for breakfast, usually made from corn meal. Dinner consisted of a small piece of beef, some corn bread, potatoes, and hominy. Fortunately, they had two cows that furnished milk and butter. 'We have no reason to Complain,' Emma noted, 'so many families are so much worse off.'

Her clothing, too, had declined in quality and quantity. She wore homespun undergarments, more coarse than they gave to slaves in prewar times. She knitted her own stockings, and a pair of heavy calfskin shoes covered her feet. Emma owned two calico dresses and a black and white plaid homespun for everyday use. She also had a few old silk outfits from prewar days which were wearing out rapidly. Those she saved for special occasions.

Each January, the community women held a bazaar at the state house to raise money for the care of soldiers. Emma helped arrange the booths. Despite the wartime shortages, the decorations looked elegant and the tables were loaded with niceties that slipped through the blockade. Cakes, sweets, and other items sold at exorbitant prices. One large doll went for $2,000. Her astonished uncle commented, 'Why one could buy a live negro baby for that!' In the three previous years, the bazaar lasted two weeks. Within four days, though, it closed because of Sherman's advance into South Carolina.

Since early January, Emma had feared for the loss of Columbia. 'The horrible picture is constantly before my mind,' she confessed in her diary, yet she refused to evacuate the city. By the time they closed the bazaar, everyone felt the city was doomed. The Confederacy had no viable force to oppose the Yankee march. Mounting anxiety reached such a peak that Emma, who always found great solace in her books, could no longer concentrate when she tried to read. The War Department ordered her father to pack up the Nitre Laboratory and move it out of danger, which left Emma, her two younger sisters, her mother, and the household slaves to brave it together.

Distant cannon booms alerted locals to the approaching bluecoats. People panicked throughout the city. Crowds, trying to flee from Sherman's path, tangled in traffic snarls. Others, like Emma, awaited the onslaught with no clear picture of how awful it would be. All those tales of brutality and destruction by Sherman's troops played on their imagination. Two days before they reached the city, Emma's sister sobbed hysterically all morning. The next day, they presented a composed front, but 'our souls are sick with anxiety.' When Union shells fell into the city, the family hunkered down in the basement. Emma felt nauseous and faint. Her mother, who had held together all that time, broke down in utter terror when she heard gunfire in the streets.

Once the Rebel cavalrymen evacuated, the shooting died down. There was a calm, and then Emma could hear shouts and finally, some Yankee troops raised the Stars and Stripes over the state capitol. 'Oh, what a horrid sight,' she wrote, that 'hateful symbol of despotism.' Emma could not look upon the Yankees without 'horror and hatred, loathing and disgust.'

That evening, the wind picked up, and by nightfall fires had begun to spread throughout the city. Smoldering cotton bales ignited by rebel cavalrymen and fanned by the high winds initiated the blaze, but Union troops, drunk on alcohol or intoxicated by their success, and fueled by their hatred of South Carolina, the hotbed of secession and in their minds the cause of this unholy rebellion, spread the flames. 'Imagine night turned into noonday,' described Emma in her journal, so bright and extensive were the fires. With hospitals that housed Union and Confederate soldiers nearby, the LeConte home escaped the ravages. Others – men and women, elderly and infant alike – did not. Except for a handful of clothing and a few morsels of food, they escaped with only their lives. The flames consumed everything else.

The inferno destroyed one-third of the city, including much of the heart of old Columbia. Charred brick walls and scorched

This is a photograph taken by George N. Barnard of the ruins of Columbia, South Carolina, from the capitol. Emma LeConte walked past this place regularly and described the destruction all around it. (National Archives)

chimney stacks were all that remained of entire city blocks. Several days after the Federal army left, Emma wandered about the town. Only a foundation and chimney remained from the old state house, where just a month earlier she had witnessed such gaiety at the bazaar. At the market, she saw the old bell, nicknamed 'secessia,' which had chimed as South Carolina and each succeeding state seceded. Now it lay half buried amid the ashes.

Emma's father escaped. He and another officer narrowly avoided capture and, after enduring considerable hardships, worked their way back home. His appearance lifted her spirits tremendously.

To feed the people, Sherman left 500 scraggly head of cattle. While many slaves took off with the Federals, quite a number stayed behind, and refugees from outlying areas flocked to the city for sustenance. Government officials, Emma's father among them, traveled far and wide in search of food to supplement the beeves. Each day, Emma drew some rancid salt pork or stringy beef and a pint of corn meal as rations.

Even though Federal troops had marched right through her state, and were at least partially responsible for the destruction of much of their city (Emma, like most locals, blamed Sherman exclusively), Emma remained defiant. She so detested the Yankees, and believed so strongly in the righteousness of the cause, that she could not imagine a just God would allow the Federals to win. She had no confidence in Johnston, who was restored to command. When she

learned he had fallen back to Raleigh, North Carolina, Emma predicted that he would retreat all the way to Lee, who 'may put a stop to his retrograde movement.' All her faith rested in Lee and his army, 'an army that has never suffered defeat, a contrast to the Western army.' When word of Lee's surrender arrived, she was so overwhelmed that 'there seemed no ground under my feet.' She resisted to the last, but Jefferson Davis's capture and the surrender of all western troops brought an end to her dreams. Her only consolation was the assassination of Abraham Lincoln, which elicited cheers from her and her family and friends.

In the immediate aftermath of the war, occupation soldiers irritated Emma, and the prospect of black soldiers overseeing them outraged her. Dreams of emigration to a different land or hopes that the next generation could wage a more successful war nourished her spirit.

Emma's father moved the family to California, where he taught at the University of California. Emma remained east. She married a Citadel cadet who entered the army with his classmates. They settled on a 1,000 acre (400ha) farm. Emma bore two girls. When the older daughter was 12, Emma's husband died. Not surprisingly, Emma ran the farm on her own and still managed to raise and educate her daughters.

Peace is declared

On 27 and 28 March 1865, Sherman visited Lincoln, Grant, and Porter at City Point. After his long travels, Sherman regaled them with tales of the trek. But this was not all fun. Grant and Sherman discussed the closing campaign, and Lincoln instructed both officers on the terms of surrender they could offer.

Before Sherman had reached North Carolina, Grant had turned Lee out of his defenses around Petersburg. Both Union generals were wary that Lee would somehow unite with Johnston and attack Sherman. With 100,000 troops, Sherman felt confident he could withstand any onslaught, but he accelerated the pace of replenishing his supplies to get his army into the field as soon as possible. The march against Johnston began on 10 April, and within two days, he learned that Lee had surrendered to Grant on the 9th. His army celebrated wildly.

Johnston had hoped that Lee could elude Grant and unite with him. While his army waited to see the results of Lee's desperate move, Johnston gathered with President Davis and other cabinet members at Greensboro, North Carolina. During the meeting, they received confirmation of the rumors that Lee had surrendered. Davis urged them to keep fighting, but Johnston announced his opposition. The people were whipped and his army was deserting in large numbers. The war was over.

With Davis's reluctant consent, Johnston contacted Sherman to open negotiations for peace. On 17 April, the two generals who had opposed each other in Mississippi, in Georgia, and again in North Carolina, assembled at the home of James and Nancy Bennett, not far from Durham Station. Sherman, forceful in war and soft in peace, offered Johnston mild terms that clearly overstepped his bounds. He permitted Confederate soldiers to take their arms home and deposit them at state capitals; he recognized state governments, restored the franchise, and said nothing of emancipation.

Had Lincoln been president, he no doubt would have corrected his general's excessive generosity. By then, however, an assassin named John Wilkes Booth had shot and killed him. At the moment when Sherman's terms arrived, Washington officials were in near hysteria. The new President, Andrew Johnson, and the cabinet unanimously rejected the terms, and Secretary of War Stanton intimated in a letter published in the *New York Times* that Sherman was a traitor.

Grant volunteered to resolve the problem. President Johnson directed Grant to supersede Sherman, but Grant refused to insult his friend that way. He traveled down to North Carolina with little fanfare and instructed Sherman to offer the same terms as he gave Lee, that they would stack arms and sign paroles, and as long as they behaved themselves and obeyed the laws, the Rebels could live undisturbed by Federal authorities. The two wrangled a bit, but Johnston, confronted with the reality of a collapsed war effort, signed on 26 April.

On 12 April, Union forces under Major-General E. R. S. Canby battled their way into Mobile. For two years, Grant had sought its capture, and as Grant ruefully noted, it finally happened when its fall meant nothing. Two weeks after Sherman and Johnston concluded the surrender agreement, Union cavalrymen captured Confederate President Jefferson Davis in Georgia. By 26 May, General Edward Kirby Smith had surrendered the Rebel forces in the trans-Mississippi west. The war was over.

On 23 May 1865, the Army of the Potomac paraded
down Pennsylvania Avenue before government officials
and huge crowds. The next day, Sherman's army, fresh
from its lengthy campaigns, marched. Sherman feared
that the dilapidated condition of his soldiers' clothing and
equipment and their broad campaign stride would prove
embarrassing in the parade. Instead, they delighted the
crowds and made their commander proud once more.
(Library of Congress)

United States

The Union army demobilized in rapid order, from one million strong at the end of the war to 80,000 men a year later. Yankee soldiers returned to their rendezvous point, received back pay, signed documents, and were officially mustered out of service. Others viewed the delay as another ridiculous government policy and simply walked home. Several decades later, when they applied for veterans' pensions, that decision proved nettlesome.

Confederate soldiers simply headed home. Men who owned their horses were allowed to take them. Some received railroad transportation as far it would take them, which in the aftermath of Sherman's marches was not usually very far. For the men from Texas, it took up to two months to make it back home.

Scholars and military experts have posited a host of reasons why the Confederacy lost. Immediately after the war, a prominent Virginia journalist and numerous military leaders blamed Southern defeat on Jefferson Davis's incapacity as commander-in-chief. Hatred of Davis motivated most of these early critics. Later scholars who attributed Rebel defeat to Davis lacked the hatred of that earlier generation. They derived their criticism of Davis largely by comparing him with Lincoln. Yet all American presidents pale whenever they are juxtaposed with Lincoln, and recent military historians and biographers of Davis have demonstrated clearly that, despite some weaknesses, Davis was certainly a competent commander-in-chief. Other students of the Civil War have argued that internal dissension undid the Confederacy, or that Southern whites lost the will to resist. But by comparison, dissension in the North was at least as powerful, and every nation that suffers a defeat ultimately loses the will to continue the fight.

In more recent years, some scholars have embraced the idea that the Confederacy should have adopted a guerrilla war. Brigadier-General Edward Porter Alexander, perhaps the most thoughtful young officer in the Confederacy, proposed the idea to Robert E. Lee in the waning days of the war. At the time, Lee rejected it, insisting that the Confederacy had borne the battle for four long years, and a guerrilla war would only extend and increase the suffering on both sides, with no real benefit. Nonetheless, a handful of historians have challenged Lee's assessment as faulty. They draw on the partisan success of the Rebels in the American Revolution, and the triumph of North Vietnam against the United States in the 1960s and 1970s. These scholars point out how vexing the guerrilla war was in Missouri, and how much difficulty the Federal army encountered in trying to protect Unionists in Tennessee and Kentucky.

Each of these views, however, suffers from serious flaws. During the American Revolution, partisans in the South performed successfully because they served in conjunction with traditional armies. Nathanael Greene and his Continentals fought alongside the guerrillas, and George Washington in New York and later Virginia commanded a standing army. By contrast with the American Revolution, which was fought in a pre-industrial era, warfare in an industrial age requires mass production, either by the nations at war or by sponsor nations that provide it to them. When a nation adopts guerrilla warfare, it exposes its people and land to enemy invasion, thereby endangering its ability to produce munitions and other materiel that are necessary for war. Vietnam received massive support from the

Soviet Union and the People's Republic of China; the Southern Confederacy had no such patron. In Vietnam, moreover, the United States imposed restrictions on where its ground troops could advance. No massive ground invasion took place in North Vietnam, and the United States only blocked supply shipments by water in the late stages of the war. During the Civil War, the Confederacy was the primary battleground, and an ever-tightening blockade, working in conjunction with land troops, had choked off imports to the Confederacy almost completely by 1865.

Selected scholars have argued that the difficulty of quelling the guerrilla war in Missouri and Tennessee demonstrates just how effective it could have been on a larger scale. But two factors undercut that assertion. First, Missouri remained in the Union, and an overwhelming percentage of its people opposed the Confederacy. Three of every four men from Missouri who entered the army donned the Union blue. Federal authorities had to deal with the people of Missouri respectfully, because so many supported the Union. Tennessee also had a strong pro-Union contingent, especially in the eastern part of the state. In other seceding states, Federals had no reason to protect the people, except for pockets of hill-country Unionists.

Second, by the late stages of the war, the Union had begun to adopt the raiding strategy, which targeted civilians and property, along with soldiers in the field, as the enemy. This was ideally suited to crushing guerrilla activities by destroying or confiscating property and making life a hell for Confederate civilians and soldiers alike. As Emma LeConte recorded in her diary, when her Uncle John, a prisoner of war, discussed the possibility of guerrilla fighting with a soldier in Sherman's army, the Yankee replied, 'Well, I hope the South won't do anything of *that* kind, for of course in that event we would not spare or respect your women.' Beneath his bluster, the soldier's comments suggested both the hardened nature of Union troops and their growing callousness toward Southern civilians. They possessed just the right attitude to combat guerrillas.

National approaches to war are products of social structure, economy, technology, and culture. Confederate whites were a propertied people, who seceded from the Union in order to protect what Mississippi called 'the greatest material interest of the world.' Their constitution attempted to secure two elements of that society, white persons and property, and they entered military service to defend both of those elements. A guerrilla war policy would have exposed their families and that property to Federal destruction or abuse, a strategy that would have undercut the very reasons for a Southern Confederacy. And by drawing food and supplies from the Southern people, while at the same time exposing their homes and property to Union destruction, Confederate guerrillas would have alienated them from the cause as well.

In organizing for war, Confederates drew on what they perceived as the Southern military tradition. They aspired to build armies along Washington's model, which would exploit martial aspects of Southern character and establish for the Confederacy a credibility with other nations of the world that guerrilla forces would not. Their heritage, secessionists believed, would more than compensate for any manpower advantages that the Union possessed.

When asked some years afterwards why the Confederates lost at Gettysburg, George Pickett replied, 'I think the Yankees had something to do it with.' That same argument best explains why the Confederacy lost the war. For all the sacrifices, for all the losses, for all the hardships, for all the narrow defeats, the Confederacy simply could not overcome the Union. Internal strife, patchy leadership, and many other factors hindered its war effort. The same, of course, could be argued for the Yankees. But in the end, the Union defeated the Confederacy; the Confederacy did not defeat itself.

Many scholars believe that the Union won because of overwhelming numbers, what one scholar has called 'the heaviest battalions.' There is truth to the North's preponderance of strength. Federals employed over two million soldiers, while the Confederacy mustered close to 900,000. Despite having one million men in uniform at once, the Northern states grew enough food to feed civilians and soldiers and still market huge amounts overseas. By the end of the war, the Union had over 700 navy vessels, many of them ironclads; the Confederacy had almost none. From November 1862 to late October 1863, the Union army purchased from Northern factories as many field artillery guns as the Confederacy's principal producer, Tredegar Iron Works, manufactured in the entire war. That same year, the Federal Ordnance Department bought over 1.4 million artillery rounds and 260 million small-arms cartridges from Northern munitions makers. For the entire war, the Confederacy produced only 150 million small-arms cartridges, and the Richmond Arsenal, the Confederacy's largest manufacturer, made 921,000 artillery rounds. Nor were these lopsided statistics simply anomalies. The same overwhelming advantages existed in weapons, clothing, and other military accouterments. But as the Vietnam experience demonstrated, overwhelming superiority in equipment, population, and even technology do not assure victory.

Ultimately, three critical factors enabled the Union to win the war. First, it possessed overwhelming resources in population, industrialization, agriculture, and transportation, and a slight edge in technology. Second, the Union benefited from political and military leaders who harnessed those resources, transforming them into military might and focusing that power on the critical aspects of the Confederacy. Finally, the Federals had a home front that remained committed enough to the war to see it through to its conclusion, despite all the losses, hardships, and sacrifices.

What were the consequences of the war? Several were obvious. More than 260,000 Confederate soldiers and over 360,000 Federals died in the war. The preponderance

lost their lives to disease. An additional 500,000 suffered wounds, and hundreds of thousands more endured ailments and disabilities from their days in the service. According to the best estimate, the total cost of the Civil War exceeded $20 billion, a figure 31 times larger than the federal government's budget in 1860. In fact, so devastating was the war to the Confederacy that it took some six decades for the Southern states to reach their 1860 level in agricultural productivity.

Once and for all time, the war removed the scourge of slavery from the American landscape. Well over four million African-Americans had been held, sold, and controlled as chattel. The war destroyed that institution. Hundreds of thousands entered Federal lines on their own. Others followed the Union armies to freedom. Still many more waited until the fighting ceased before securing their liberty. Passage and ratification of the Thirteenth Amendment to the US Constitution, abolishing slavery forever, made certain that wartime measures freeing slaves could not be overturned in peacetime.

While the achievement of freedom was a wondrous thing for blacks, white society prevented them from exploiting its benefits fully. The Fourteenth Amendment secured citizenship and equal protection and due process of law. The Fifteenth Amendment granted black males the right to vote. But in time, Southern whites resurrected their power and stripped African-Americans of many of their rights. Northerners, tired of war and struggles over power in the South, yielded Southern control to Southern whites. Although African-Americans in the South and the North were better off after the destruction of slavery, it took more than a century for them to achieve their Civil War goal of basic civil rights.

By winning the war, too, the Northern vision of the United States took precedence over the more local, states' rights, agriculturally oriented version of the South. No longer were they states united, but a United States. The federal government established its preponderance over the state governments, a trend that has continued ever since. The nation moved on an accelerated course of industrialization and urbanization. And finally, the Northern version of freedom, with aspirations of egalitarianism and economic opportunity for all, prevailed for white Americans.

Although Southern whites howled over Reconstruction policies, they were under the circumstances quite mild. There were no wholesale land confiscations, no widespread imprisonments, no mass executions for treason. Only Major Henry Wirz, Commandant of Andersonville Prison, was put to death. Among Rebel leaders, Jefferson Davis alone was held in jail for two years, but Northerners never had the stomach for a trial. After his release, Davis lived a long life in the United States. By 1877, the US government had removed all soldiers from the former Confederacy, and the last of the secessionist states had returned as full and equal partners in the Union.

After the war, word circulated that the great Prussian general Helmuth von Moltke had said of Sherman's army that there was nothing one could learn from 'an armed mob.' When asked about it, Sherman replied that he knew Moltke but never questioned him on the story, 'because I did not presume that he was such an ass as to say that.'

From a military standpoint, the Civil War offered an extremely valuable legacy for thoughtful analysts. American military leaders realized that rifles, artillery, and field fortifications weighed heavily on the side of defenders. Over the next few decades, US army officers sought to restore the tactical offensive to warfare through single-line formations with greater dispersion and mobility, to reduce the impact of defensive weapons.

Most European analysts dismissed the war as one conducted by bumbling amateurs. They insisted that breech-loading small arms of the late 1860s made lessons from all previous wars obsolete. In the minds of most foreign experts, the lightning offensives and decisive campaigns of the Austro-Prussian and Franco-Prussian Wars readily cast a dark shadow over any insights into future

conflicts from the American Civil War. Yet the Civil War proved more prophetic of the First World War than either of those clashes between European powers. Analysts failed to grasp the enhanced power of the defensive and the value of good field works. They also missed valuable lessons from cavalry serving as mounted infantry, a combination of mobility and firepower that proved so decisive in the Second World War.

Lieutenant-General Philip Sheridan, the hard-charging general who had arrested a corps commander for arriving with his men 12 hours late, observed the Franco-Prussian War from the Prussian side. In a letter to Grant in 1870, he thought that the battles were actually not that distinct from the Civil War, and 'that difference is to the credit of our own country.' Sheridan believed, 'There is nothing to be learned here professionally, but it is a satisfaction to learn that such is the case.' He insisted that Europeans could benefit from studying Americans' more effective use of cavalry and rifle pits, better protection of their lines of communication, and more efficient staff departments. By the end of the century, some European officers had extracted valuable lessons from studying the Civil War, particularly tactics, but not enough to anticipate the unparalleled bloodshed in the First World War.

Little more than a month before his death, Lincoln had called for the nation to complete its undertaking and then bind its wounds. Several decades later, survivors on both sides attempted to do just that, to set aside old grudges and to shake hands at several battlefield commemorations. In their youth, they had been touched by fire. By middle and old age, that passion and animus had largely flickered out. And while veterans retained many fond memories, and preferred to emphasize those aspects in their letters and conversations, they never forgot the harsh side of war.

In 1864, an Illinois officer assessed, 'There is no God in war. It is merciless, cruel, vindictive, un-christian savage, relentless. It is all that devils could wish for.' Few veterans would have disagreed.

Further reading

Primary sources

Basler, Roy F., ed., *Collected Works of Abraham Lincoln*, 8 vols, New Brunswick, New Jersey, 1953.

Davis, Keith F., *George N. Barnard: Photographer of Sherman's Campaigns*, Kansas City, Missouri, 1990.

William W. Edgerton Papers, University of Houston.

Grant, U. S., *Personal Memoirs*, 2 vols, 1885.

LeConte, Joseph, *'Ware Sherman: A Journal of Three Months' Personal Experience in the Last Days of the Confederacy*, Berkeley, California, 1938.

Miers, Earl Schenck, ed., *When the World Ended: The Diary of Emma LeConte*, New York, 1957.

Record Group 94, National Archives.

Sherman, William T., *Memoirs of W. T. Sherman By Himself*, 2 vols, New York, 1891.

War of the Rebellion: Official Records of the Union and Confederate Armies, 128 vols, Washington, DC, 1880–1901.

Secondary sources

Bailey, Anne J., *The Chessboard of War: Sherman and Hood in the Autumn Campaigns of 1864*, Lincoln, Nebraska, 2000.

Ballard, Michael B., *Pemberton: A Biography*, Jackson, Mississippi, 1991.

Bearss, Edwin C., *The Vicksburg Campaign*, 2 vols, Dayton, Ohio, 1985–86.

Boatner, Mark M., III, *The Civil War Dictionary*, New York, 1959.

Bradley, Mark L., *Last Stand in the Carolinas: The Battle of Bentonville*, Campbell, California, 1996.

Castel, Albert, *Decision in the West: The Atlanta Campaign of 1864*, Lawrence, Kansas, 1991.

Castel, Albert, *William Clarke Quantrill: His Life and Times*, New York, 1962.

Connelly, Thomas L., *Army of the Heartland: The Army of Tennessee, 1861–1862*, Baton Rouge, Louisiana, 1967.

Connelly, Thomas L., *Autumn of Glory: The Army of Tennessee, 1862–1865*, Baton Rouge, Louisiana, 1971.

Cooper, William J., Jr, *Jefferson Davis, American*, New York, 2000.

Coulter, E. Merton, *The Confederate States of America, 1861–1865*, Baton Rouge, Louisiana, 1950.

Cozzens, Peter, *This Terrible Sound: The Battle of Chickamauga*, Urbana, Illinois, 1992.

Daniel, Larry J., *Soldiering in the Army of Tennessee: A Portrait of Life in a Confederate Army*, Chapel Hill, North Carolina, 1991.

Davis, William C., *Jefferson Davis: The Man and His Hour*, New York, 1991.

Fellman, Michael, *Inside War: The Guerrilla Conflict in Missouri During the American Civil War*, New York, 1989.

Gallagher, Gary W., *The Confederate War*, Cambridge, Massachusetts, 1997.

Glatthaar, Joseph T., *Forged in Battle: The Civil War Alliance of Black Soldiers and White Officers*, New York, 1990.

Glatthaar, Joseph T., 'Lord High Admiral of the US Navy,' *Military History Quarterly*, vol. 6, no. 4 (summer 1994), pp. 6–26.

Glatthaar, Joseph T., *The March to the Sea and Beyond: Sherman's Troops in the Savannah and Carolinas Campaigns*, New York, 1985.

Glatthaar, Joseph T., *Partners in Command: Relationships Between Leaders in the Civil War*, New York, 1994.

Hattaway, Herman, and Jones, Archer, *How the North Won: A Military History of the Civil War*, Urbana, Illinois, 1983.

Lamers, William M., *The Edge of Glory: A Biography of General William S. Rosecrans, USA*, Baton Rouge, Louisiana, 1999.

McMurry, Richard M., *Atlanta 1864: Last Chance for the Confederacy*, Lincoln, Nebraska, 2000.

McPherson, James M., *Battlecry of Freedom: The Civil War Era*, New York, 1988.

Marszalek, John F., *Sherman: A Soldier's Passion for Order*, New York, 1993.

Marvel, William, *Andersonville: The Last Depot*, Chapel Hill, North Carolina, 1994.

Roland, Charles P., *The American Iliad: The Story of the Civil War*, Lexington, Kentucky, 1991.

Simpson, Brooks D., *Ulysses S. Grant: Triumph Over Adversity, 1822–1865*, Boston, Massachusetts, 2000.

Sword, Wiley, *Embrace an Angry Wind: The Confederacy's Last Hurrah: Spring Hill, Franklin and Nashville*, New York, 1992.

Symonds, Craig L., *Joseph E. Johnston: A Civil War Biography*, New York, 1992.

Symonds, Craig L., *Stonewall of the West: Patrick Cleburne and the Civil War*, Lawrence, Kansas, 1997.

Wiley, Bell I., *The Life of Billy Yank: The Common Soldier of the Union*, Indianapolis, Indiana, 1952.

Wiley, Bell I., *The Life of Johnny Reb: The Common Soldier of the Confederacy*, Indianapolis, Indiana, 1943.

Woodworth, Steven E., *Jefferson Davis and His Generals: The Failure of Confederate High Command*, Lawrence, Kansas, 1990.

Index

Other titles in the Essential Histories series

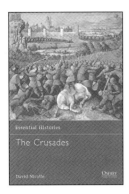

The Crusades
ISBN 1 84176 179 6

available

The Crimean War
ISBN 1 84176 186 9

available

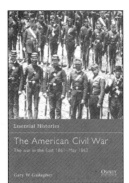

The American Civil War
The war in the East
1861–May 1863
ISBN 1 84176 239 3

available

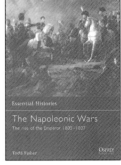

The Napoleonic Wars
The rise of the Emperor
1805–1807
ISBN 1 84176 205 9

available

The Seven Years' War
ISBN 1 84176 191 5

available

The American Civil War
The war in the East
1863–1865
ISBN 1 84176 205 9

available

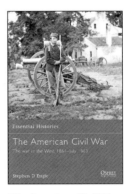

The American Civil War
The war in the West
1861–July 1863
ISBN 1 84176 240 7

available

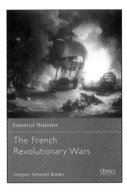

**The French
Revolutionary Wars**
ISBN 1 84176 283 0

available

The Korean War
ISBN 1 84176 282 2

available

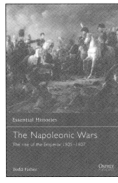

The Napoleonic Wars
The Empires fight back
1808–1812
ISBN 1 84176 298 9

available

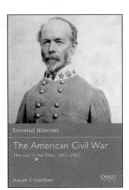

The American Civil War
The war in the West
1863–1865
ISBN 1 84176 242 3

available

The Norman Invasion
ISBN 1 84176 228 8

available

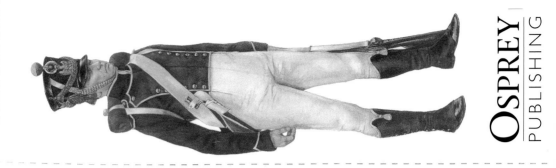

FIND OUT MORE ABOUT OSPREY

❏ Please send me a FREE trial issue of Osprey Military Journal

❏ Please send me the latest listing of Osprey's publications

❏ I would like to subscribe to Osprey's e-mail newsletter

Title/rank

Name

Address

Postcode/zip

State/country

E-mail

Which book did this card come from?

❏ I am interested in military history

My preferred period of military history is _____

❏ I am interested in military aviation

My preferred period of military aviation is _____

I am interested in (please tick all that apply)

❏ general history   ❏ militaria   ❏ model making

❏ wargaming   ❏ re-enactment

Please send to:

USA & Canada:
Osprey Direct USA, c/o Motorbooks International,
PO Box 1, 729 Prospect Avenue, Osceola, WI 54020, USA

UK, Europe and rest of world:
Osprey Direct UK, PO Box 140, Wellingborough,
Northants, NN8 2FA, United Kingdom

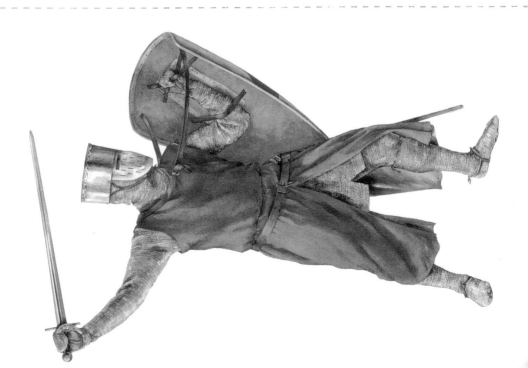

OSPREY
PUBLISHING

www.ospreypublishing.com

call our telephone hotline
for a free information pack

USA & Canada: 1-800-458-0454
UK, Europe and rest of world call:
+44 (0) 1933 443 863

Young Guardsman
Figure taken from *Warrior 22:*
Imperial Guardsman 1799–1815
Published by Osprey
Illustrated by Christa Hook

POSTCARD

Knight, c.1190
Figure taken from *Warrior 1: Norman Knight 950 – 1204AD*
Published by Osprey
Illustrated by Christa Hook